PRAISE FOR JUSTIN NEVIN'S APPROACH

The stakes were high, the word counts low and, to make matters worse, I had not written a story about myself since elementary school. Luckily, Justin Nevin was there to help coach me through the process of writing college essays. His techniques and exercises encouraged me to see the stories buried in seemingly ordinary events and to write about them thoughtfully. His exacting approach to language and focus on reflections rather than conclusions continue to inform my writing.

—Claire Perry, Haverford College, class of 2014

This book really helps to cultivate the techniques necessary to write a successful college essay. It doesn't just refer to techniques to incorporate into an essay; it actually shows you how to make these techniques effective. It has an excellent way of showing students how to expound on essays they have already written, and of helping them to begin an essay from scratch.

—G. K., Swarthmore College, class of 2017

To put it simply, I wouldn't have gotten into my alma mater without the help of Justin Nevin. I got accepted early, received a substantial scholarship and, when I met my admissions officer, he mentioned that my essay was what made my application really stand out from the crowd of other applicants. Justin's writing advice was invaluable and helped me on my way into college and beyond.

—Jenn Lapp, University of Southern California, class of 2014

Princeton offered early action admission to my son, and our family couldn't be happier with the results. Words cannot express our deep appreciation and gratitude for all Justin's professional guidance and valuable advice. Not only did he help get him on track with the essays, but he inspired him by giving insight into college life. I reread his Princeton essay, and I know it is my son.

—*D. O., father, Princeton University, class of 2016*

Writing college essays is such a daunting task. Justin taught me how important it was to tell a story and evoke emotion to stand out from the crowd. Justin's writing tips helped get me accepted into every college I applied to, including competitive schools such as Ohio State, Boston University, and Penn State. His lessons and techniques are truly invaluable and helped get me to where I am today.

—*Amanda Chiodo, The Ohio State University, class of 2017*

Justin has a good sense for the college essay, but more importantly, he has a good sense for prospective students. He was a good partner for Carolyn in helping her hear her own voice. And it was great to sit back and let the process work with Justin's support!

—*Karen P., mother of Carolyn, Emory University, class of 2018*

Justin played a critical role in helping to revise my college essay by pushing me to construct a tight and fluid argument that did not constrain my ability to creatively express myself. Beyond succeeding in writing an effective college essay, my experience with him allowed me to overcome the challenge of putting into words what was ultimately an incredibly personal story of self-discovery.

—*Robbie Trocchia, Vassar College, class of 2014*

"IS IT EASY BEING GREEN?"

WRITING THE NEW COLLEGE APPLICATION ESSAY

JUSTIN NEVIN

Published by Sourcebooks, Inc.
P.O. Box 4410, Naperville, Illinois 60567-4410
(630) 961-3900
Fax: (630) 961-2168
www.sourcebooks.com

Library of Congress Cataloging-in-Publication Data is on file with the publisher.

Printed and bound in the United States of America.
VP 10 9 8 7 6 5 4 3 2 1

For Lauren, Henry, and William

CONTENTS

INTRODUCTION

THE PERSONAL ESSAY:
A CREATIVE ALTERNATIVE TO THE
FIVE-PARAGRAPH ESSAY

AMERICAN HIGH SCHOOL STUDENTS spend so much of their education writing five-paragraph essays. Yet the formality and structure of academic essay writing leave little or no room for personal exploration. When asked to write about themselves—what they're passionate about, how their past experiences have shaped them, how they envision their futures, and even whether they think it's easy being green—students often have no model to draw on or structural equivalent to the five-paragraph essay to follow. And that's what makes the college application essay, at the heart of which lies personal exploration, so challenging and intimidating for so many students.

Some schools have always asked unusual essay questions. Now the essay questions lobbed at students range from the plain to the increasingly strange at more schools, and seem to coincide with augmented international interest in American colleges and universities, increased American applications across state lines, and an uptick in the average number of schools that American students are applying to. American schools—particularly the most selective ones—are turning away candidates with test scores, GPAs, recommendations, and activity profiles similar to those of students who are accepted. With only so many factors to consider, admissions officials are putting more emphasis on the application essay to distinguish highly qualified students from each other. Quirky essay questions and the expanded word count of the new Common Application (CA4) personal statement both speak to this emphasis.

It is with this emphasis in mind that this book adapts the established genre of the personal essay as a structural equivalent to the thesis-driven academic essays that high school students are used to writing. Here *structural* does not imply a fixed number of paragraphs. Rather, as you read more about the personal essay, you will find that the methods presented in this book are simple enough to apply immediately to your writing yet dynamic enough to enhance your essays substantially. In short, this book aims to familiarize students with the wonderful and open genre of the personal essay, to give them greater confidence and a stronger foothold in their college admissions essays. By introducing applicants to useful specifics of this rich genre, I hope that readers will sidestep the frenzied race that college admissions has become by simply focusing on practical ways to maximize the short space they are typically given to write about themselves. Importantly, the new Common Application prompts are ripe for the personal essay, which will allow you to present a key part of your admissions profile in a creative way that appeals to a wider array of schools.

A compelling personal essay can also provide a strong foundation that you can easily adjust to answer other school-specific, supplemental, or optional essays that may be part of some colleges' applications. This book does not go into great detail explaining how to answer any given college's prompt because a well-crafted personal essay can be both specific and flexible enough to meet the demands of *many* different types of application questions, however conventional or unusual they may be. By following the guidelines here, you will likely be able to use or modify only a few essays to meet the application requirements for all your schools.

What Makes This Book Different

This book offers the unique advantage of an anthology of essays in Part I, combined with in-depth explanations of how to implement the modeled techniques in your writing in Part II—features that would typically be found in two separate books on writing the admissions essay. Instead of being grouped by theme, these essays are arranged according to the organizational concepts that they illustrate. All these essays put to use more than the one concept for which they're categorized, so as you read, you will begin to pick up on these concepts even when they're not pointed out directly. The appendices briefly present advice on related admissions factors like brainstorming, time management, teacher recommendations, the admissions interview, and athletic recruitment. In short, the basic idea behind this book is that better engaging with the admissions process will bring better results.

The essays presented here have been chosen for their sophistication, not necessarily because they were admissions essays—they are meant to challenge your preconceived notions about what an admissions essay should or should not be. Some richly detail everyday events, while others forcefully explore sensitive personal material. These sensitive essays are included for you to consider what you are comfortable sharing with prospective schools. Perhaps you have been advised not to write about negative personal material—certainly, you might choose not to write on such a topic. But as you read the essays collected here, consider what they have in common beneath their widely ranging subjects. If you can't relate to a particular essay, then put yourself in the seat of an admissions officer. Ask yourself what you can glean about that writer and how he or she successfully uses the personal essay to provide a complex portrait in a short writing space. If you do have sensitive personal material that you want to write on, you should feel encouraged and prepared to do so.

Second to breathing, telling stories is the most natural thing we as humans do. Intently engaging in narrative writing will connect you, person to person, to more admissions readers in the most fundamental way. This is the only book to provide specific guidance on writing personal essays for college applications.

Time Is on My Side

When you're busily studying and participating in extracurricular activities, you might scoff (understandably) at the notion of taking your time, which is why it is best to start working on application essays the summer before your senior year and shepherding them to controlled completion when applications are due in the fall. Think of writing your college essays as a hobby and treat them as an end in themselves. In fact, forget that they are even college essays. Write essays. The more time you give yourself to explore personal expression in writing, the more you will enjoy the process and the better essays you will write.

Depending on how you learn and write, you might get more out of this book if you have at least one college application essay underway (however rough or incomplete). If you have not begun drafting your essays, choose a prompt from a college you might apply to or from the Common Application (see Appendix 1: Essay Questions You Might See) and take half an hour to write a response on your own—or simply write an essay on a personal experience without using a prompt. As you continue reading this book, you might find some writing techniques are more difficult to use than others. With time and practice, from draft to draft and application to application, these points of advice will make their way more and more naturally into your writing. Ultimately, though, you should focus on what is most useful to you. An extended timeline for the application process can be found in Appendix 4: Timelines for Applying.

I'm under the Gun

If you are a high school senior reading this after, say, the beginning of December, odds are that you have at least one application due in the coming week or two. (In fact, some colleges' early applications are due November 1.) In any case, the deadlines pile up quickly, and if you are feeling squeezed for time, see Appendix 4: Timelines for Applying for a condensed but controlled application timeline. By following this recommended path, you should still be able to get a grip on the basic organizational techniques needed to write a controlled personal narrative in a short amount of time, even if you can't afford the luxury of taking extra time to plan, draft, and revise.

Remember, many, many high school students before you have had to whiz through the application process while managing the demands of school, family, work, or sports. Even though the process might seem overwhelming now, it will be over before you know it.

And you'll do just fine.

PART I
ESSAYS

NARRATIVE ESSAYS:
THE STORIES WE TELL

THIS BOOK FOCUSES ON two modes—or ways—of writing. The first one is narrative—storytelling. And most importantly, this storytelling is done *in the moment*. In other words, instead of attempting to tell his or her life story, each of the authors of the following essays focuses on one or two moments to explore richly. The essays in this chapter illustrate the uses of action and dialogue, the two most important techniques for establishing narrative in the personal essay. While narrative is the central organizational mode for the personal essay, it is also something that you can use as much or as little as you'd like. That is, narrative elements like action and dialogue can be excellent tools for starting off an essay that goes on to explore and reflect in lyric mode (see Chapter 2), or your essay can start in narrative and continue like this to the end. As you read this first group of essays, keep an eye on how the authors use action and dialogue to keep their narratives focused and under control. Although each essay here successfully delivers a strong narrative, storytelling is used in different proportion by the authors (see Chapter 6 for more on proportion).

Even where the authors don't state outright what these events mean to them, what can you infer from their respective choices of narrative action and dialogue? How does the choice of writing about one event or the other characterize each author, in your opinion? Narrative allows the admissions reader to answer these questions by staying actively engaged with your essay. Instead of stating outright the importance or value of an experience, these authors largely let their narratives do the talking for them.

As you read this first set of essays, ask yourself what kinds of prompts each could answer. For most prompts that you encounter in college applications, narrative is the way to go regardless of the specific topic. By focusing on telling a controlled story, your essay can be used or modified to answer prompts for several schools' applications.

Off the Table
Anonymous

In my first year of lessons, the half-hour car rides my dad and I endured to and from the club were awkward and silent. I, with my headphones plugged in, listened to the smooth jazz licks of Herbie Hancock to avoid the wall of silence that formed between our seats. After hundreds of trips, lengthy car rides to tournaments, and seemingly endless cross-country plane rides, that wall of silence between us began to wither.

Out in the Tennessee heat, I plopped myself on a bench. I had lost matches before but never with so much at stake, and especially in such a big upset. Then my dad took a seat beside me and put his hand on my back. He did not look happy. Then again, he did not look angry either, or even disappointed. He just—looked at me in a calm and casual manner.

"I'm not an expert, but I can tell you one thing about that match. You looked scared. Not nervous, but scared," he said. Shockingly, I was not bitter when he pointed out my flaws so bluntly. Indeed it was that moment when my dad became my perception of what a father should be. Unlike before, he did not approach the situation by trying to change the topic. He talked to me with full genuine attention, and that is when I finally recognized our assimilation into American culture and realized how far we had come as a family. The language and cultural barriers that came with being

Korean immigrants had posed innumerable problems for us and made growing up in America more difficult than it should have been. Up until that point, we dealt with those problems by either ignoring the struggle or by simply accepting the complacency of not adapting. With those passive methods, we suppressed our emotions. Bonds between us stretched thin, and conversations grew short and superficial.

Most importantly, vulnerability was missing. Family members should not have to struggle to share their emotions with one another, but I fell victim to this. I had a lot to say. However, I knew that even if I were to share my feelings and thoughts, my parents would not be able to reciprocate, and not from a lack of love or a lack of parenting ability, but because they were inherently rooted in a different culture. For most of my childhood, my parents and I did not share the same linguistic and cultural threads with which to stitch this problem together. That turned around when I started playing table tennis. My parents' traditional Korean values no longer clashed with my progressive American upbringing, and our two languages no longer got jumbled together, for table tennis became our focal point and our common language. The sport gave us excuses to be together on those long drives, allowed us to be trusting and—most importantly—emotionally vulnerable, and with that common point of reference between their past and my present, we were able to grow.

(Word count: 501)

I Can't Tell You
Sean Thammakhoune

My dad and I are on our way to Canobie Lake Park, an amusement park near my town. It is a small one, but it holds over a week's excitement to any small ten-year-old boy. As we drive there, I think about all the rides. I love riding them, but seeing how they work is what keeps me coming time and time again. I often stand below a roller coaster to see the angles to be able to finish the track with only the force of gravity, or try to calculate how fast a ride has to spin in order for a person to magically stick on the wall.

With the excitement building up inside of me, I start thinking of all the rides that I am about to embark on. There must be a new ride that I can examine while zipping through its track. I think of asking my dad what we are going to see at Canobie, but I know that he probably will not tell me. He is a rather secretive person. I know that he is super passionate about his work, because he is almost never home. This is a rare occasion that I get to spend time with him, and I could not be happier. He does not tell me much, and I have come to expect that. But I am a very curious young boy, and I love to ask questions. Sometimes I think I begin to annoy him. All the excitement causes me to blurt out a question that I have wondered for years.

"Hey, Daddy, I have a question for you. A serious one. What exactly do you do at your workplace? I know you're an engine-ear, but what do you do?" I ask, thinking that there is a slight chance my dad designed a new ride.

"I build stuff. For the military, you know. I'll show you what I mean when we get to Canobie in a few seconds. We're almost there, I promise. I can't tell you right now, but I will tell you this: we protect those who protect us," he replies.

I knew it. Canobie has a new ride that my dad built, and I can fly it like a jet, or maybe drive it like a tank. I rest my head back and relax, knowing that when I awake, I will be a small walk away from riding the best ride ever. When we arrive at Canobie, there is a twinkle in my eye. It is Military Day at the park, a day to showcase the vehicles used in combat. F-22 Raptor fighter jets are lined up in front of the roller coasters as if they are ready to take off and go into action, creating a breathtaking scene. The size, the flashiness, the slick design all stand out in the ray of sunshine gleaming off of the jets. The large desert-toned tanks stand tall in front of the jets and tower over us. I can feel intimidation completely drape over me, even though I know I am in a safe place. Suddenly, a stealth bomber flies overhead, and it feels like a war is about to initiate, and we are the helpless civilians caught in the middle. Once the crowd realizes that we are in fact safe, we let out a sigh of relief mixed with amazement.

We proceed to the tanks, the epitome of intimidation. I climb inside, my dad pushing my rear end so I can get high enough to grab the seat. The sophisticated controls catch my attention immediately, as I mash buttons left and right. I think of my dad's previous answer. A spark ignites that fuels my passion for engineering. My dad pokes his head in, and I ask him if this is what he does, but he just smiles and takes my hand to leave.

(Word count: 650)

Fenway
Lindsey Luker

Thirty years from his glory days, the hockey player in my dad still shows. His eyes are constantly scanning, his foot placement is purposeful and smooth, and his shoulders are always tense, locked and ready to bear a hit. He walks a few steps behind me as we step onto the field to join thirty other people, also decked out in Red Sox apparel. My dad squeezes my shoulders and says, "This is it, buddy. This is Fenway."

People fight and push to get a look at the players. I spin on my heels and feel my heartbeat quicken as I search the crowd for my dad. I finally spot him away from the other fans, right along the first base line, bending over with his elbows on his knees where the dirt meets the grass. He's at the very edge of where fans with field passes are allowed, the red velvet rope to his left containing us. His brow is furrowed as he examines the border between green and brown. His defined calves and forearms are tanned from hours of golf. His oversized collared T-shirt hides his growing belly, the result of our endless Oreo supply. He grabs his mouth and the scruff around it with his right hand, his wrinkled forehead frozen in puzzlement. I trot toward my father, still enthralled. "Thought I lost you for a second there, Dad. What's so interesting down there?"

He pushes himself up from his elbows, steals one more glance at the grass, and looks around. His eyebrows are almost touching the tips of his short eyelashes. He scratches the back of his head with his thick, square fingers. "I heard you can't even touch this grass, but I don't get it. What's the point of this spectacular stuff if it can't be walked on?"

I follow my dad's eyes. They pause, ever so slightly, at each of the field officers located around the park. They are young men, likely in college, who line the field dressed in their cargo shorts and white collared shirts. I roll my eyes. "Dad," I whine, "let's not cause a scene. There's nothing wrong with flying under the radar." But the sparkle in my dad's eyes tells me it's too late. His dull blue eyes have come alive in the sun and the scheme, begging for an accomplice. He takes a quick look around him, sees no security, and steps out of his faded moccasins. He looks at me again, grinning, and ducks under the security rope that separates the dirt from the grass. Five feet onto the coveted grass, I see him wiggle his toes around in the bright green blades. He bends down nonchalantly to pluck a few from the field. My eyes and mouth hang equally wide. He makes his way toward home plate, savoring every step in the sacred grass. My dad, chest out and shoulders wide, is intercepted by a young man, probably twenty, with bright blue eyes and hair so blond it's almost white. I can feel my face heating up and small tributaries of sweat sliding down my back.

"Sir," he says in his deepest voice, "I'm going to have to ask you to get off the grass. You can't be on it unless you're authorized." My dad doesn't move a step. He's leaning forward, just a little, and his arms hang casually at his sides. The security man glances longingly at my dad's feet, imploring them to carry this crazy man off the grass. After a manly stare-down, my dad chuckles a little, shakes his head, turns, and walks to his shoes. He reaches into his pocket, grabs the few blades he had managed to smuggle, and tosses them with a flick of his fingers back onto the field. The boy hangs his head sheepishly, unable to form a sentence.

(Word count: 643)

Rosalie's Move
Mary R. Becker

My best friend Rosalie said, "Helmethead"—her nickname for her father—"has cancer, and I'm moving to Florida on Monday." It was Friday.

When Rosalie told me her news in that joking tone a person only uses when dangerously close to coming unhinged, there was a question in her eyes with their vulnerable depth and in her voice as it dropped off.

I blinked away the tears before they could form and uttered, "How can I help?"

After cleaning and packing everything, down to little pink caps for her cat's claws so that she would not scratch the furniture, Rosalie, Helmethead, and I went to Market Basket to pick up groceries. As he grabbed a cart, Rosalie's father asked me what groceries they needed because he knew that I would know. I panicked. At that moment, I realized just how deep into their lives I was. I kept asking Rosalie what she wanted to eat for dinner, but she could not say.

That day when she told me about her impending move and her father's cancer, something snapped into place inside of me. I had a purpose, a chance to prove my strength to the world, a friend in need, a place to do good. I stopped seeing Rosalie as a friend and started seeing her as something to be fixed. But I did not have the tools to solve all of her problems, and it was driving me mad.

Rosalie did not move to Florida after all because her father did not get the necessary papers signed by his ex-wife, Rosalie's mother. I never got out of that protective mode and never stopped trying to help her.

After spending a week with Rosalie and her father on vacation in California, on the way back home, Rosalie said, "The car will be so comfortable after that plane." The first thought that popped into my head was, *at this point a coffin would be more comfortable.* For once I was glad for Helmethead's maniacal driving. I reminded him to put on his seat belt as we flew out of the parking garage, the sound of horns fading behind us.

After the trip to California, I wrote Rosalie a letter. I told her I couldn't see her anymore because I could not help but try in vain to help her. My goal was to make her happy, and sometimes I achieved it for a brief while, but I could not change what caused her trouble. A few days after I stopped trying, she moved to a town a couple of hours away.

I saw her one more time—at our school's biannual jazz café. We hugged and chatted as if we were in front of a water cooler exchanging empty invitations. She hugged me. It struck me how slippery she was. Before, when we used to hug, she would hold onto me as if I was the edge of a cliff.

(Word count: 491)

Slightly Off Key
D. G.

While I was practicing a classical Beethoven piece one sunny afternoon, the way the sunlight reflected off the shiny chestnut brown of my Yamaha piano lit up a previously unexplored portion of my psyche, one that said, "Hey, why not just futz around a bit?" I couldn't resist the urge. For a second, then a minute, and then an hour, I emptied my mind of the minutiae of classical compositions and just let my feelings flow, first into my fingers and then onto the black and white keys. The result was original if not impressive; it opened up a new musical path for me full of spontaneity and discovery.

A few years later, comping the last B-flat seventh chord in the phrase, my synapses fired as I prepared for the Kingda Ka of jazz solos. That final "One, two, three, four" and the slight pause of anticipation before my fingers flew across the keys, and then the ride began. The freedom within the structure was the ultimate reward—the way I could deviate from the typical B-flat blues to surprise myself with combinations of chromatic fills and scales beyond my wildest imagination.

My first experience with creative enhancements was less than auspicious. In second grade, my teacher assigned us a Thanksgiving Day project. She gave each of us a metal form to use for our papier-mâché turkeys.

"Just wrap the paper around the mold like this, and your turkey will appear," she said.

As my fingers touched the damp, sticky sheets of newspaper coated with paste, I had an epiphany. I would make my turkey with two heads! Like Cerberus in the Greek mythology books my parents read to me at night, my turkey would have supernatural powers. I rolled up some extra paper, stuck it in the mold, and made a second head for my turkey.

"Did you hear my instructions?" my teacher inquired.

"Yes, but I had another idea, about a turkey with two heads."

My teacher called my parents later that afternoon. She mentioned "difficulty following instructions," and my parents later told me that, sometimes, you just need to color in the picture instead of making a picture of your own. Yet they also told me they were proud of my artistic "improvements," even if they made my papier-mâché Thanksgiving turkey almost unrecognizable.

Despite my teacher's concerns, the two-headed turkey might just have a positive legacy. In doing *New York Times* crossword puzzles with my grandmother, I see that discovery isn't only about filling in squares. The real discoveries are made when we think outside the boxes themselves to solve those elusive Sunday-puzzle clues. And in thinking innovatively, I've had to ask some big questions, ranging from the scientific "How can this DNA mutation be avoided to prevent cancer?" to the much more personal "Why am I different and why does it matter?"

Moreover, every time I listen to John Coltrane's "My Favorite Things," I am reminded that my life is slightly off key. As a gay individual and jazz musician, I've learned to accept and embrace the different tones, extending the basic chords from ninths to elevenths, using the disparities as a source of strength instead of seeking resolution in simple harmonies.

(Word count: 536)

LYRIC ESSAYS:
INVITING THE READER IN

THE ESSAYS IN THIS chapter contain some narrative elements, but their appeal lies in the emotional impact of the authors' reflections—lyric writing. So you might find some action and dialogue, but these narrative elements generally aren't used in the moment. There is instead a softer quality about how these authors interpret their subjects. They might write more generally about events, habits, or observations without grounding them in a particular narrative moment. Rather, you might say that they hover around or above central ideas, turning them over to reflect on them from different angles as the essays progress.

Writing in the lyric mode can offer a rich exploration of a subject or idea beyond the concrete actions and bits of dialogue in a narrative. To do so successfully means that there is something *in you* that you haven't figured out yet. The lyric space can be one in which you figure things out as you write—there's a sense of discovery at the end.

The key to a successful lyric essay is to write with this sense of surprise and discovery, as opposed to making statements that assign explicit value to your subject. In other words, the way you write about your subject might be as much of a surprise to you as it is to your reader. Statements that close off this sense of open discovery belong to commentary, which neither deepens lyric reflection nor advances narrative (see Chapter 7 for more on commentary). While rich, creative language is always important, lyric essays especially rely on creative uses of language for their success, particularly because time is suspended without the use of narrative. This means that lyric essays can be strategically "slower" than narrative ones. Instead of tracing the progress of an event, imagine that your reader is jumping from one insightful and creative expression to the next to make his or her way through your essay.

Lyric essays can be used to answer virtually any admissions prompt. Whether you use primarily narrative or lyric in your essay will depend on the topic you choose and how you feel about it.

Toes
Megan Walcek

I saw my grandmother only twice a year, but in those two visits, I noticed how she noticed things. She could always tell which contestant was about to get the Daily Double because that was the only time Alex ever said the word *answer* before asking the question. When mixing a pot of mac & cheese, she reassured me that it didn't matter when I foolishly added too much milk, since I could just let the soupy mess sit a couple more minutes and the noodles would absorb it as if I had never made the mistake at all. One day she looked at my feet and told me I had nice, long toes.

I had never noticed my toes before. Well, I'd never really looked at them in the way she had. I had lived with those toes for seventeen years—cursed at them when I stubbed them, crinkled them when someone tickled them, and adorned them with an array of metallic OPI nail polishes—but never once had it occurred to me that I had "nice, long" toes.

I think of my grandma at my age, seventeen, and wonder what she noticed then. She was living the comfortable life of a typical teenager—much like mine, I imagine. Around that period in time, her parents made her discover something new about herself too, something she must have sensed all along but never acknowledged before—her innate courage and strength. They did not tell her that she was strong. They did not foster her development as she grew up, or spoon-feed her through her late teens. Instead, they died. And in the next five years, she became the mother to her younger siblings, a wife, a pregnant widow grieving the loss of her husband, and a single parent. Did she notice her strength?

After my grandmother died five years ago, I started noticing things about myself too, similar to the way she had seen my toes. I noticed how my eyes were never really the same blue—sometimes they were a gray-blue, sometimes a true blue, and sometimes I was not convinced that they were really blue at all. I noticed how my right thumbprint swirled counterclockwise (I think that means I'm going to have three kids). I noticed that as much as Dr. Thomas tried to close the gap, my two front teeth still did not completely touch.

Seventeen years I had lived with my eyes, my toes, and my thumbprint, but never before had I noticed them; seventeen years my grandma lived with a hidden strength inside of her. Unlike her, I have not yet encountered true adversity. My own inner strengths have not yet been tested. It is human nature to fear inadequacy when faced with challenge; however, viewing my grandmother as a model has transformed my fear into curiosity. What have I yet to notice about my own capabilities? What inner strengths do I possess? Regardless of the obstacles that await me, I am confident that such strengths exist. I know they are ample and I know they are more than adequate.

(Word count: 518)

Everyone's Story
Ethan LaFrance

On a drizzly September morning, I swayed to "This Land is Your Land" with three hundred people in a small park near my home. Some of us held signs; some of us made speeches. We were protesting an attack. A block from the park, someone with a Sharpie pen and a closed mind had scrawled a racist phrase on the home of a family from Somalia. In the quiet neighborhoods of Concord, New Hampshire, neither racism nor protest is supposed to happen, but now both had. I am an activist. For as long as I have relished reading history and the newspaper, I have wanted to change the world.

It began years before, when my family moved to Concord. My father and I set out to explore the neighborhood park but stumbled while trying to push my brother's stroller on a crumbling path. Soon, my father was making phone calls, forming a neighborhood committee to restore the park, and planning a winter carnival. Watching him, I learned that living in a community meant filling the cracks you found.

At school, this lesson led me to cofound a mentoring program that matched upperclassmen with at-risk ninth graders. Through this program, I met Jacob, who couldn't afford the calculator he needed in Algebra I. Poor eyesight, no glasses, and the feeling that he didn't "belong" in the front of the classroom kept the white board out of sight. When I learned this, I knew that Jacob's challenge was mine as well. One calculator, a pep talk, and many conversations later, Jacob was in the front of the classroom, working his way toward an A. With Jacob, I realized that leading meant inspiring people and learning from them in the process.

Last year, I read an essay that began, "I felt like a psycho prisoner from Mars." Through his words, Samir, my partner in a writing class, brought me on his journey from a refugee camp in Nepal to the halls of our high school. Together, we decided to "be the change." Teaming up with a social worker, Samir and I organized a weekly group lunch. Over spicy fries and chocolate milk, students got to know each other as fellow skateboarders, readers, music lovers, and people. Samir taught me that diversity tested our ability to look past labels and to find the humanity in everyone's story.

Standing in the park, gripping a microphone, I told the crowd how we didn't have a community for us all until we valued the story in each of us. Growing up, reading about leaders who bent the arc of history, watching my father better our neighborhood, and listening to the stories of people in my community have shaped me. When leaders and stories inspire action, they fill cracks and change the world. Through learning and leading, I can do just that.

(Word count: 476)

The State of the Art
Ian M. Jesset

Love forms the strongest bonds: love of God, love of country, love of composers. Two of my best friends love a man named Stephen Sondheim. He is a most brilliant composer and lyricist. Over the course of about a year, I observed my two friends, Jade and Mike, bonding over how great a genius Stevie was. At the time, I really liked a couple of things he'd written, so every now and again I could join in the bonding. I finally decided to agree that Stevie was a genius (I'm very stingy about calling people geniuses). I began listening to more and more of his music and became faster and faster friends with these two. All of us took great joy in reciting his difficult, wordy lyrics as quickly as we could and in admiring the depth of insight he gave on everyday life. I got my music from Jade and Mike, and one Sondy CD was entitled *Sunday in the Park with George*.

I fell head-over-heels in love with the concept. It was about the French painter Georges Seurat and his art, and the nature of art in general. Specifically, the show is about *A Sunday Afternoon on the Island of La Grande Jatte*, a pointillist masterpiece. Pointillism is a style of painting in which dots of pure color form all the figures. The musical style of the show reflects the visual style of pointillism. Yes, that is the genius of Stephen Sondheim: that he can take a visual style and make it into music. A key point in the musical is how Seurat creates distance from others by his obsession with his work and his meticulous personality.

The more I listened to this music, the more important the painting *A Sunday Afternoon on the Island of La Grande Jatte* became to me. I realized that I could see myself in this artist's shoes. I could see that I was often caught up in little details and missing out on the outside world, and I could see that I had no artistic passions and was not trying to say anything with the things I created. I knew that I didn't want to have a whimsical art; seriousness of purpose was important to me.

So now I even keep a copy of the painting in my bedroom, where I can always look to remind myself of the way little things make the whole, but that there is a risk in watching them too closely, and of the order and beauty of a Sunday afternoon off. The painting also recalls, if I may quote my favorite composer, that "Art isn't easy./Every minor detail/Is a major decision/Have to keep things in scale,/Have to hold to your vision."[1]

(Word count: 460)

Family Matters
Ian M. Jesset

"Let the Wookie win," says C-3PO to R2-D2.[2] The advice is sound. Let the people who really care have their way, especially when you think that the situation is trivial. This advice has been given to me in story form since the early days of my youth. The advice usually comes from my father, telling me about my mother.

You see, my mother is a very competitive person; my father, however, is very relaxed and loose about competition. The let-the-Wookie-win tales tend to follow the basic form of this one: "Your mother and I were playing basketball with some of our friends, and she and I were on opposing teams. Well, the game was pretty close, and your mother, while going up for a rebound, punched me in the face. I needed stitches on my upper lip."

Now, this punch was accidental, and I do believe that my mother would never in a million years purposely hurt anyone in her family. But the point is that people who really want things go out of their way to get them, sometimes accidentally punching a face or two on the way. This has certainly been advice I try to follow.

"Well, duh," you're probably thinking. "Why have an unnecessary

---

1. Stephen Sondheim, "Putting It Together," *Sunday in the Park with George*, Warner/Chappell Music, 1990. Citations made for references in any students' essays are for the publication of this book. Typically, simply alluding to the source of your direct quotation or paraphrase is just fine for application essays. Just like with academic essays, you want to make sure that you quote correctly and properly acknowledge your source. Beyond this, though, the rules are more relaxed for admissions purposes.

2. *Star Wars*. Directed by George Lucas. Lucasfilm, 1977.

conflict?" And that's, I suppose, a valid point, but I think that that kind of "well, duh" moment gets overlooked a lot. Imagine, if you will, all the "well, duh" thoughts in the world. I think that first you'll notice there is an awful lot of them, an *awful lot*.

The question then becomes, does taking this advice actually correlate with being weak-willed? I don't know the answer to this question with any degree of certainty; after all, graceful yielding can be seen as kind or as weak. But I believe there is a difference between weak-willed and kind. The distinction between kind and weak-willed tends to be a purely situational one with no strict way to tell by definition. Thus we would say that it is kind to let someone else have the last doughnut since you've had some, whereas we would say it was weak-willed to let someone else take the last doughnut when you've had none and they've had enough already.

So may we then say that if you have enough and let others take what you would have in excess, this is an example of kindness or of a weak will, but that if you are lacking and let someone else take in excess you can only be seen as weak-willed? Not necessarily, because many people say that Gandhi was kind, and he often went without while letting others take in excess. You wouldn't say that Gandhi was weak-willed either.

Thus, if we consider Gandhi strong-willed and lacking necessities but generous, we can say that having a weak will has no correlation to kindness. At least, no correlation based on the facts presented here.

(Word count: 487)

Splitting Wood
H. Charles

Growing up in suburban Illinois, I had little experience splitting wood. The trees in our neighborhood were scarce and stunted, and I couldn't point to a single person who burned wood for heat. Then, seven years ago, in the dead of winter, we packed up and moved to northern New Hampshire. Wood-burning chimneys sprouted from rooftops everywhere. Our new house had *two* wood stoves, a fireplace, and an almost empty woodbin. In the first year, when the splitting maul was still taller and heavier than I was, my father served as chainsawer, wood splitter, and pile stacker, working through our first grapple-load of logs entirely on his own. Eleven years old, I watched intently and made wishful mental notes.

As I grew and matured, I became a cog in the wood-splitting machine—albeit a minor one. I progressed as does a martial artist: learning each step carefully, mastering precise movements, moving incrementally forward with each chilly autumn day. My apprenticeship began with the second grapple-load, carting small piles of cut wood from the top of our driveway to the back of our house so Dad could stack them. I was eager to split on my own; it was evident—even to a teenager—Dad needed help. Eight cords is no small amount. Picture a school bus turned on its side, the wheels removed and the front end lopped off. Eight cords is *a lot* of wood. But my dad was insistent: I was to be a carter and no more.

With the arrival of the third towering stack of trees, I was ready to graduate to the next level. Finally I could wield the maul and split alongside Dad. I had no idea what I was getting into.

Splitting wood is tough. It takes more than bulging muscles and a sharp ax or weighty maul—in fact, I doubt some of the strongest men alive could split a hardy New Hampshire log. Splitting depends on precision, timing, and a sharply focused mind. For me, it's a meditative process, a thinker's art. The first time I tried it, I swung the maul as I'd seen Dad do it thousands of times; the maul hit the top of the log and literally bounced. A shudder shot through my hands and set my whole body shaking. "Well, your *technique* wasn't bad," my dad volunteered. My splitting career had begun.

A certain mood—quiet, calm, peaceful—comes over me when I feel like splitting. When it strikes, I go to the garage and gather up the trusty maul. The handle is cool to the touch, but it warms quickly as my hands mold to the smooth wood. Sometimes I throw the maul over my shoulder—if someone is watching, I want to look strong. Sometimes I simply let it hang—a clear sign I'm feeling tired. At the pile, I grip it with both hands, one near the base and the other near the head, "shaking hands with the coworker," my father calls it. The maul and I get reacquainted, like old friends.

Some perspective: the pile *looms* over our driveway. And it has to be split and moved. Now, I'm certified to do this on my own. Before I begin, I find the perfect chopping block. I search for a block that calls to me—a large and battle-scarred old man, a solid and uncomplaining base. I roll him carefully to a pre-cleared patch of ground and "table" him—tipping him on one flat end. At this moment I enter what can only be called "my inner self." I begin to talk to myself, talk to the logs, talk to the world.

Muttering, I scavenge the pile, hunting for my first target. It is usually a youthful log, an easy split. I lift it to my chopping block and stand it on end. A small crack in the log's center lines up with the center of my body and the maul's blade. I focus, almost willing the log to fall apart. My base widens; I shuffle my feet. The maul's head drops low, nearly scraping the pavement, and then, in a contained fury, arcs high over my head and strikes downward. The force of the blow powers into the log, cleaving it into two neat halves.

I should be honest here: as a wood splitter, I'm still learning. Sometimes, I'm utterly foiled by a stubborn, seemingly unsplittable log. It rejects the maul like I've been rejected, on occasion, by a pretty girl. And then there are times when the maul wedges itself happily in a log and refuses to budge. (So much for coworker cooperation.) Generally, though, I like it. Splitting wood has built me up: it's made me more resilient, more reflective, and even, maybe, a bit more relaxed. Years from now, when I'm living in Southern California, or Miami Beach, or on the French Riviera—anywhere where wood-burning chimneys are nonexistent—I'll look back and smile, knowing that through all the mis-hits and sore forearms and not-so-silent curses, I actually enjoyed myself. Perhaps I'll even have a winter house to retreat to, and a pile of logs.

(Word count: 858)

FACT VS. TRUTH:
WHAT OUR EXPERIENCES MEAN

FOR MANY WRITERS, FACTS are the building blocks for a creative personal essay. While we all understand that facts are an inescapable part of life and of storytelling, we also experience how limiting facts can be in trying to express some deeper truth that we feel. Indeed, the facts of a story don't always add up to this truth. To attempt to get at a deeper truth, writers can find themselves working against or around facts that can't bring to light the inexplicable, the strange, or the unbelievable. Some things are beyond comprehension, either because of what they are when they occur or because of who we are when we witness or learn about them.

The essays in this chapter illustrate how the personal essay can be extremely useful for exploring topics that are by their nature unclear. Sometimes the "truth" that a writer finds is very different from the mere facts that make up a story. And this truth might also hold a more personal value for the writer than it does for others. The exploration of this difference can lead to a more creative essay because the essay works as a whole to get across to the reader—to gesture at—this truth that might be hard for the writer to articulate or to face directly.

Essays that take on the fact-truth difficulty can be narrative or lyric in structure or a combination of both. Application prompts that ask you to write about disappointments or challenges you have faced can be ripe for this kind of exploration.

Where Fault Lies
Emily R. Fernandes

I sat in the pew staring up at the pleasant-looking priest. Words of the responsorial, gospel, homily all rushed by my ears. I could not focus on the words; my mind was fixed on the man at the end of the altar. I was studying him, concentrating on his appearance, looking for a glimpse of the man described in the papers. I scanned his face for traces of lust, longing, or perversion, but I saw only the kindly and paternal priest you would want looking over your parochial school.

It was the beginning of fourth grade when my school's parish was given a new priest, sent to us by Bishop Malcolm. Father Jeff stood about five foot five and sixty pounds over weight. He was a short roly-poly man who brought to mind thoughts of your lovable old grandfather. He had a little terrier he walked through the playground. Yet when he walked through the courtyard full of children, he seemed too eager to please. Even in fourth grade, I felt that something was not quite right.

Gossip is a driving force in a small school. Even at staunch St. Peter School, hearsay rattled up and down the halls. But when rumors flew that our new priest was less then virtuous, I was shocked. Later we learned that he had paid a young man to sleep with him; this lasted for three years. This young man, now over the age of eighteen, stepped forward and spoke to a local newspaper while Father Jeff was acting as St. Peter School's priest.

When the rumors were confirmed, hell broke loose. Children were pulled out of Masses, parents held meetings, and protests were formed, and the recipient of this wrath was Bishop Malcolm. Everyone reacted differently to our church's betrayal.

Teachers ignored it and refused to speak about it. Parents were enraged and demanded that he resign. I was petrified. I sat through Mass pinned to my pew in fear. When I was required to go to communion, I prayed profusely that I would not receive from him.

Although I was terrified of Father Jeff, I did not blame him. I was scared of what he did and what he was, but I could appreciate what led up to his fatal downfall. While his intentions were not honorable, they were understandable. I could not comprehend Bishop Malcolm's actions. To send a priest who had been so tempted to preach at a school parish is like sending a wolf to protect sheep. He well knew of Father Jeff's past. Over one hundred children could have been emotionally scarred, and for what reason? What was the motive for his actions?

I still think of Bishop Malcolm, although he has become a shapeless form. He is an elusive shadow, a sound in the dark. He is more of a symbol to me than an actual person, a symbol of pain that can be handed down quickly and with no thought. I often wonder if he ever felt blame. Did he ever consider this a sin? When in such denial, how can one see truth? When in such denial, how can one show sympathy? In such denial, how can one feel guilt?

(Word count: 538)

Taking Steps Forward
Brianna B.

I slouched over with my back against the oak door of my parents' bathroom, observing the room that remained remarkably untouched by time. Two years ago in this very room, my sister Maggie committed suicide. I still remember it like it was yesterday; ambulances and police cars from every surrounding town filled my driveway and spilled out onto the dirt road. My family and I were not allowed into our own home for several hours, and when we finally returned, everything reeked of bleach from the cleaning crew. No matter how much bleach was used, though, the pain and the heartache could not be erased.

I had spent fourteen years of my life following in Maggie's footsteps and learning from her mistakes, and when she was gone, I struggled to find my own way. I remember a conversation I had with her only a few short weeks before her death as we huddled in the blankets of my twin-sized bed. According to my alarm clock, we had been talking for almost four hours, but the darkness masked the passage of time. Tears ran down my cheeks as she whispered how she had been having all these horrible thoughts, but a small piece of me managed to believe her when she promised, "I will never leave you alone."

After she had broken the one promise that ever mattered to me, I found myself at a crossroads. It would have been too easy to give up and give in to the tragedy that life had thrown my way, but I knew that that was not what Maggie would have wanted for me. She would want me to push forward and achieve all that she never had the chance to; she would want me to live.

Even in my sister's passing, she will always be my inspiration. When I was in sixth grade, Maggie's appendix ruptured and she was flown to Dartmouth Hitchcock Medical Center for emergency care. I silently watched the doctors and nurses rush to save her life from the corner of the hospital room, thanking God for their hard work and devotion. Ever since then, it has been my dream to become a doctor so I can give someone else a second chance at life, just as those doctors had done for Maggie. Six years later, I am more determined than ever to make this dream a reality.

Instead of letting her death break me, I have let it give me motivation to work that much harder for everything I do. It may be easier to give in and wallow in self-pity, but that will never be who I am. I am a fighter, and even though there will be days when I struggle, I will always have my sister to look up to in those difficult times. I now have faith and confidence in who I am and who I am going to be; after all, I am living for more than just myself now, but for Maggie as well.

(Word count: 504)

Running
Michaelle Yeo

1. The postcards that you bought just outside of the Colosseum and paid too much for are taped sloppily to your closet door. They are not quite your memories because the sky was never that blue—it was

a rolling pane of fogged glass, soaking and permanently darkening your sneakers with Roman mud and rain. You reach in the closet to grab a pair of socks. You step out of your room, slipping on the darkened sneakers. For those few inevitable moments, you remember the heavy air tasting of smoke, the white tips of the Vittoriano rising between the gray sides of buildings at every turn, your aching legs. You step out onto the porch. The sky is blue, cloudless.

2.   Her name is Sam. She sits by the side of the road every day, except on the weekends, warming her heavy stomach against the asphalt, tail wagging limply. Some days, her owner calls to her, walking up the dirt path to the road, always in a flowered print, waving a well-loved Beanie Baby to coax Sam back into the house. You wave as you walk past. She squints, smiles, waves. You begin to jog a little as you see the green shadows of the trail you run stretch from just around the corner.

3.   Pebbles roll, twigs snap. Ke$ha throbs in your ears, pounds in your head. Feet fall in cadence with a breathing that you know is not yours because you are somewhere in that cloudless sky, lost.

4.   Your sneakers leave creased marks in the soft sand, a path, fading even now, coiling among clumps of pine needles and abandoned beach toys. The small strip of beach curves up into a concrete path to a boathouse of red, knotted wood and a dock, tipped slightly on its side. The waves roll and break against the rocks. You sit for a moment at the edge of the concrete, panting, beads of sweat on your forehead, watching the sun pool into rivulets of orange and magenta and violet, trickling out from behind the gray, swaybacked clouds. In the distance, two mated loons skim the surface of the rising waves, black flecks bobbing against sky. Cooing, heads bobbing, they salute the setting sun and each other's rising wings.

You kick off your shoes, feeling the grains of sand shift beneath your feet and then suddenly the unfamiliar kiss of the cold waves. You savor this moment because this will not just be a memory caught in a skewed snapshot from someone else's lens. It is a postcard of your own, addressed to somewhere you don't yet know.

(Word count: 438)

Larger Than
Jac Stewart

After the planes crashed into the towers, I drank a juice box. Then I had math class. Then I went to physical education. We marched to the gym single-file. The hallway was quiet and familiar, the wood-paneled floors glossy in the fluorescent light. Fifth grade was just like fourth. My new classroom was right next door to my old one. Mrs. Lewis was excited in her striped spandex pants. She had a new game for us. We threw big rubber bouncy balls at each other. The balls stung when they hit you, but there were safe zones to hide in. Nobody could hit you in the safe zones. The game lasted about forty-five minutes. Some time while we were playing, I guess, Mrs. Lewis went quiet. But that was the only change. She went on smiling. I didn't notice she had stopped shouting her usual instructions until later. The game was pretty fun. Nobody cheated, and my team won. I was thinking about the rules and the strategy for most of the day.

Nobody said anything about terrorists until Celia's mom met us at the bus stop. She said two men had flown airplanes into the World Trade Center. The World Trade Center in New York. It was a place where important business deals happened, and the businessmen there had briefcases. Important people with important briefcases. It was sunny out. Not too hot, either. Nice puffy clouds. Good weather. Terrorists had killed a lot of these people, she said.

I had heard of "terrorists" before. Mom and Dad would mention them once in a while, when the TV told us about something they'd done. I understood the important facts about the terrorists. First, they were always men. I did not know how or when this was decided, but it definitely had been decided. Next, they had beards. This may have been why they were only men. The beards might have been critical. And they blew things up. Just to hurt other people. That was a terrorist. There were a lot of them, but only in the small desert countries sort of near Europe. As I walked home by myself, I thought I saw one of them crouched in the dark spot between two trees. A shadow in the garage made me jump because I thought I saw one of those bearded Middle Eastern men waiting for me there with a hunting knife.

When I opened the door to the kitchen, I could hear the TV playing in the next room. I'm usually the first person home. So I walked over to the TV room. Mom was crying in one of our comfy red chairs. On the screen, a tower was smoking. It fell down. My mom cried for a long time. The news anchors were sad too. Carson Daly from *Total Request Live* was sad. Everything on the TV was American flags and serious faces. It made me sad to see everybody so unhappy. After a while, we got up, and Mom drove me to swim practice.

I thought I should get to skip practice because of the attacks. But we had it anyway. I changed, talked about video games with that Tim kid, tiptoed over the little tiles to the edge of the pool. Just like every other week. We swam laps. Over and over again, in silence. The instructors, Jan and Paula, sat on the white lip of the water, picking at their swimsuits. Neither of them mentioned the Trade Center, but they were wearing the serious faces I saw on TV.

Mom picked me up in the empty parking lot out front of the YMCA. We ate dinner with my brother and my dad. Lasagna. It was okay. I did some spelling homework and went to bed. The next morning, Mom was in the kitchen when I came downstairs. Like usual. But the TV was on, and everybody was still talking about yesterday's news. They were even replaying that video of the first tower collapsing, like they wanted Mom to cry again. That weird ripple moved so slowly through the building, toward the ground.

No matter what channel I went to, they were talking about the airplanes or showing a field in Pennsylvania or exchanging the serious face from faraway cities. I didn't get why somebody would want to hear about the terrorists anymore. Maybe on September 11, but it was September 12. *TRL* was supposed to be for music videos again. The Backstreet Boys weren't going to attack me in my garage. They probably didn't even own hunting knives. "Larger Than Life" had good robot suits and good choreography. It always played out the same way. First, there was a spaceship launch, then each band member's adventure, then a dazzling dance routine featuring all the members of the group. It was predictable. Cool. The spaceship's flight was always successful. The only buildings were shiny and futuristic—they didn't ripple or shudder or even shake. I figured people were still calling in, demanding "Larger Than Life." Mrs. Lewis had probably planned a new game, with instructions she would shout nice and loud in another pair of spandex leggings. They should've played the video.

(Word count: 867)

Bar Fights in the Future
Jac Stewart

By 2013, everything in my life will be perfect but pleasantly realistic but awful and meaningless. These contradictions slink around in the murky place in my head reserved for imagining the future. Many of them predict mutually exclusive events, like getting hit by a school bus and wandering in the White Mountains, taking place at the same moment five years from now. Reality will force these options into the linear march of time, but I dream in systems of equations. Actually, I wouldn't even call them dreams. The term implicitly excludes nightmares, a critical player in my arithmetic fantasies. For every time I envision graduating college in 2013, I see three or four instances of bad luck, idiocy, or mediocrity derailing my life at the same juncture. My brain is a bar fight among an idealist, a realist, and a surrealist. When the wild-eyed dreamer is pinning the other two on the pool table, I picture myself in the woods. I have a beard and I'm wearing flannel semi-ironically. The beard is thick, and it impresses everybody, but I don't grow it for them. It relates to some high ideals I've yet to flesh out as I lope about the most isolated parts of the forest. Rest assured, though, that they're important ideals. I'm going to express them really well in an epiphany on top of a mountain when some significant symbol from my past (a childhood friend or maybe something quirkier, like my grandma's Saint Peter candles) suddenly reveals itself to me from the shadows of nature.

The surrealist is weak from insomnia and stress but more reckless than the others for the same reasons. He thrashes his body violently until he escapes the idealist's grip then quickly pulls a rope out of his pocket. After he lassos his enemies, he ties the cord tight around them and loops it around and around, binding their arms to their sides. I sit watching television in a dirty white room. No one else is there, but unlike in the woods, this just makes me lonely. My beard is dirty and pathetic, more a few days' scrubby bristles than real facial hair. My arms flail uncontrollably, but they are held steady by a straitjacket. Even the jacket is dirty and white. The television mumbles about diet pills. I try to remember something, anything from the past five years, but all that I can think of is the smudges of grime streaked on the walls.

But the realist is by far the most experienced of them all with drunken brawls. He wriggles free from his ties and seizes his two foes. He slams them up against the dilapidated bar, clunking their heads against neighboring taps. My vision changes. I am in the Midwest studying history in the sensible corn/wheat/something fields of Minnesota/Ohio/Wisconsin. I'm pretty happy. It's cold outside without my flannel shirt and superhuman will. But I hum along contentedly, doing my homework. Later, I will drive to the supermarket alone to buy my microwave dinners. The beard is slightly patchier, less impressive. I'm okay with it. The something fields are buzzing with life, and I start to smile, but the idealist and surrealist quickly overcome the realist again and everything is chaos in my barroom. Their battle will rage on interminably, leaving pieces of all three of them lying on the ground for reality to work with.

(Word count: 570)

REDUCTION AND STYLE BEFORE CONTENT: MAKING PEOPLE INTO CHARACTERS AND LEARNING TO LEAVE MATERIAL OUT

F ROM THE TIME WE are infants, we depend on the adults around us for physical and emotional growth. As we grow and mature, these older figures can take on new and changing values for us because we become different people too. For better or worse, these roles are reversed, disrupted, or changed. Yet as we become young adults and establish our own identities, adults who have been in our lives since we were small—parents, grandparents, other relatives, coaches, teachers, community leaders, friends' parents—might still seem "too large" as personalities to get a grip on in the personal essay. The essays in this chapter manage to "reduce" important figures in their authors' lives to manageable characters on the page. This form of reduction helps writers decide what is worth keeping in the personal essay and what can be done without.

Ultimately, style is a matter of writing well about what you do choose to keep in the essay, instead of writing down everything you want to say. How you reduce these people in your life will have a large impact on how you are able to manage the content that goes into your essay. By carefully choosing the traits of the people in your essays, you can more effectively control your style.

These guidelines apply to any essay, whether lyric or narrative or both. If you are struggling with how to convincingly depict key personal figures in such a short writing space, reduction and favoring style before content can help you manage better (see Chapter 8 for more on these tools).

Some Fancy Name
Lauren G.

A brand-new Mercedes in my driveway was the first thing I saw upon arriving home from school. Even though I couldn't drive it, getting anything new and shiny as a kid was exciting. Nonetheless, I was confused. Dad had just purchased a new car, and I always heard my parents talking about how money was tight.

Dad's vein-popping yell was unmistakable. I could hear it before I even walked through the front door. My excitement morphed into anxiety and fear. I didn't want to see what I already knew was behind that door.

"I'm ready to call the divorce attorney!" were the first words I heard. My mother was beyond furious. Apparently, her reaction to the new car was not the same as my own. My father, looking oddly bewildered, herded my brother, my sister, and me upstairs to the safety and calmness of our rooms. I sat curled up, listening to what was being said downstairs. According to my mom, Dad was missing all day and she had been very concerned. When she saw the car, her worry became intense anger. I was too young to realize that his actions and sporadic emotions were not normal for a mentally stable adult. After what seemed like an eternity, the yelling finally stopped with a door slam.

I reluctantly made my way back downstairs to see my mom sitting on the bottom step, hunched over. I could hear the faint sound of her sobbing. I sat down next to her and tried to console her—taking her side as I always did—but she told me it wasn't my job to make her feel better. I asked where Dad had gone but she didn't know. She got up to make dinner, and I went to go join my brother and sister in watching TV. When my mom called us in for dinner, my dad's usual spot at the table was empty, and remained empty.

After dinner, I heard my mom talking to somebody on the phone. She said that Dad must have been off his medicine. I had no idea what she was talking about.

Around nine o'clock, I heard the garage door open and my dad walked in. Worried about where he had been all night, I felt relief sweep over me. I watched my parents go into the other room and shut the door. They were clearly having some secret discussion that was not appropriate for us to hear. When they came out, it seemed that they had made up, for now at least.

My mom came to say good night as she always did. "Why did you forgive Dad so fast?" I asked. "I've never seen you that mad before."

This made her stop and think. She sat down on the edge of my bed. "Daddy can't help his actions," she said. "There's something wrong with the way his brain works."

She didn't give me some fancy name for his problem, but everything made much more sense.

(Word count: 502)

Standing up Alone
Manda Marie

The last rays of sun slide through the blinds in my cousin's square, sea-foam green hospital room. I sit in the chair-bed beside Sarah with my worn and creased paperback copy of *Pride and Prejudice* open across the knee of my wrinkled jeans. Sarah sleeps peacefully now, and I search for the hiss of her breath and the beep of the EKG machine to be sure that she is alive while my eyes skim across sassy dialogue between Elizabeth Bennet and Mr. Darcy.

Two weeks earlier, I sat next to my aunt in the stiff-backed chair of the waiting room, reading an article about Angelina and Brad and their plans to adopt another child. The doctor swung the door open and set Sarah free into the waiting room but hesitated a moment before beckoning my aunt into the office. Sarah flittered around the room picking up toys, with the end of her blond ponytail hanging from the side of her mouth—an old habit she couldn't seem to break. I followed along behind her, placing each item back in its correct place as she told me about the whooshing of the "MR an' I scanner," as she called it. My aunt's piercing scream from the next room interrupted her. I slid my fingers into Sarah's and squeezed. Her palm was like a dead fish, cold and sweaty against mine. My aunt emerged with furrowed brows. The car was silent on the way home, and my lips almost bubbled with questions I wanted to ask. I refrained. My aunt told me the news first, in the linen closet surrounded by crisply folded bed sheets and fuzzy towels: Sarah had a hair ball the size of a grapefruit in her stomach.

When I was ten and she was twelve, I could tell there was something about Sarah that separated her from the rest of the school kids. The other kids didn't like Sarah, and therefore didn't like me sometimes. One day I caught the end of a conversation about her while walking out to the playground. Peter Howe, a boy in her grade, called her a retard. I didn't know what the word meant—it didn't matter—but I still received a detention for pushing him.

In sixth grade I discovered Google. Google gave me 1,241,746,483 results for a search of "children who act younger than actual age." The list was endless as I scrolled down with the white mouse of the school's Mac computer. The first result was a website on the diagnosis of a child with Asperger's syndrome. Sarah matched seven of the ten descriptions.

I sit alone with her in this hospital room, but this is nothing new. We are alone, even when there are fifty other people around us. Always alone. At family gatherings, cousins cordially tolerate her when parents are present, but as soon as they turn their backs, we are ignored or harassed. Sarah is too oblivious to notice their malice, but I used to be infuriated. I would try to "get back" at them. The few cuss words that I knew burned like acid as they left my lips. These callous expressions never changed anything, though, not for them, not for us. We stayed together; they stayed together. It isn't really us against them; it just seems it. Her parents bicker in hushed tones about me—how long I should stay and, oh, how they wish I was her. Their voices are just loud enough to carry through the vents. My mother accuses me of being "too tolerating" when I ask for a ride to Sarah's house; I ride my bike instead. None of this matters because nothing will change it, not as long as I still sit here in this hospital room, almost alone.

My eyes wander to the clock: eleven o'clock. I snuggle into the chair and pull the hand-knitted afghan over me. Mr. Darcy asks Elizabeth if she will stay this time; she does.

(Word count: 665)

The Stairs
David F. White

I am staying up late tonight. I spent all night doing my homework, and just when I was about go to sleep, oops, the TV somehow turned on. *The Daily Show* starts in ten minutes, so I should probably watch that. And there is no way I'm missing *The Colbert Report* either. Anyway, it's too late, and I don't feel like getting criticized by my grumbling parents in the morning when I sleep past the screeching alarm. Luckily, I have my own personal alarm system: the stairs. The stairs tell when my parents will make their final ascent of the day and retire to their room, allowing me the freedom to deprive myself of my much-needed sleep.

My stepfather is the easiest to identify. It is his house, and he walks with authority, especially while stomping up the stairs. His repetitive and predictable *thud, thud, thud* thunders through the house. I don't know if he is aware just how loud his steps are, but nobody is going to tell him to be lighter on his feet. As soon as he walks out of the kitchen into the foyer, I know it's him. With one swift motion, I turn the TV off and wait for the moment when he slams the bedroom door behind him.

My mother is much more discreet. Her steps are timid, yet firm, as she strolls around the house in a quiet shuffle. The friction between her feet and the carpet creates a soft *swish, swish, swish*. This barely audible tone gives me just enough time to click off the TV. I hope she doesn't see the sudden white flash as the screen goes black. Yet, soon enough, I hear the door shut and the affirming click of the lock.

In my house, the stairs are the centerpiece that glues everything together. Showcased in the foyer, the twelve steps separate the social space of the downstairs from the private sanctuaries of the bedrooms above. The carpet, once a bold off-white, has been trampled and matted into an ambiguous beige. Dirt speckles every crease and corner, finding the best place to hide from the occasional vacuum cleaning.

I know my stairs so well that I am able to wander up or down the steps in the daze of a midnight awakening, even in total dark. Or in the rush of forgetting my phone or iPod before school, I can climb with speed and precision, to save myself from being late, without ever tripping. Sometimes, I feel daring enough to skip a step, thrusting myself upward with the help of the railing.

My steps change with my mood. After a long day, I make my final climb with a timid and tired step. After a bad day, I take out my frustration on the stairs, punishing each with a powerful stomp. On those days when I'm at ease, each step has a similar pace and pattern. My legs move forward and lift up in a continuous, fluid motion. One step after another, I march in silence. My stride has my rhythm, and each step upward gives my home a pulse of life.

(Word count: 525)

Twice as Nice
Michael H.

"Where the hell did you come from?" The startled older lady gawked at me. "Didn't I just see you over there?" The lady looked back and forth quickly toward the gardening display and then became noticeably fixated on the shirt underneath my work vest.

"Ma'am, I've been at this register all day," I told the lady.

From the gardening section came another voice: "Ma'am, you dropped something out of your basket."

The lady looked frantically back and forth again. "There're two of you!" she exclaimed loudly.

That lady hasn't been the only person surprised to see my twin Shaun and me both working at the same store. Most customers are just a little surprised and entertained, but many customers are confounded, like they just saw a giraffe walk in.

"I thought for a minute there you changed your shirt. Your hair looked funny too." The lady was excited at her realization that we were twins. However, it's always funny to wonder how a person can logically think someone changed their clothes and haircut less than a minute after seeing them the first time.

"Ha-ha, that's so great," she said happily. She then slipped in a joke I've heard almost every single day since I started working: "I guess I'm seeing double!" She giggled and winked at us before leaving, convinced of her originality and cleverness.

Shaun and I gave each other an understanding look as the lady walked away. We both knew what each other was thinking, and that had nothing to do with extrasensory perception.

Usually, I never think about having a twin. It can be a great icebreaker and there are a few other minor perks, but it's so normal to me that it usually never crosses my mind until an elderly lady is shocked by it. But it's difficult not to feel awkward when it is brought up, because only one of two things could be happening: either we're being grouped as the same person, or compared as opposites.

If someone meets us for the first time, they automatically view us as an entity, a single pair rather than individuals. It is a strange feeling to be thought of as being exactly the same as another person, especially when I understand how decidedly different my brother and I really are. This point of view is also quite common to anyone who has to buy us birthday presents (or present).

Unfortunately, it is even more awkward to be seen as totally opposite from your brother, as many of my friends do. There are always comparisons made about the two of us, and inevitably there is no way for others to avoid preferring either Shaun or me when they do so. Nothing can make me more self-conscious than repeatedly comparing me to my own brother.

Whoever is favored in the argument, I feel horrible that one of us is seen as slightly inferior.

Other than these awkward moments, having a twin is simply the opportunity to have a closer, more understanding friend than one can possibly dream up. And that certainly makes up for the gawking old ladies.

(Word count: 524)

Missing Work
Spencer Pallas

The report cards were passed around the room. It being math class, I wasn't too worried. Math had always been my expertise and came surprisingly easily to me. I looked over the paper nonchalantly, not expecting to find much. After looking over the page a couple of times from shock, I ran up to the teacher's desk. "Is there something wrong here?" I asked her, positive that a little mistake had knocked my respectable B average to an F. She carefully looked it over and looked in her book and also in her computer. "Everything looks right to me," she said with a condescending tone. "That's what happens when you don't do your homework."

I was in utter shock. I had always done my homework; it was something I prided myself on. I looked at her blankly and told her that I had done all of the assignments. "Well, I don't have them; did you check your bag?" Already knowing that they were not there and had been handed in on the due dates, I reluctantly rummaged through my bag. Nothing, big surprise. "Well, if you don't like the grade, then do them over for half credit" was her only remark. Now these were not everyday, a couple of problems here, a couple of problems there assignments. These were big, in-depth, graph-covered, multiple-page assignments. I stomped back to my seat in anger.

There was nothing I could do; it was my word against hers. The fact that she was alive when Jesus was a boy didn't help my case. She was past her prime and lost things on a regular basis but would not take my word for it. After devoting one of my only weekends when I didn't have to work to math, I was able to get them all redone. I always tried to portray a little feeling in my homework, even in math, but these assignments were as dry as the Sahara. My grade was brought up to a C—still not great. We went through the rest of the quarter, me having to work even harder to bring the grade back up to a more respectable mark.

It was one of the last days of the quarter when she called me up to her desk. Ever since this little incident, I had never really "felt the love," as some may say, from this teacher. On her desk was the original stack of my homework that I had supposedly never turned in. "I found them and you will get full credit." That is all she said to me. Not "Spencer, I'm very sorry for putting you through all of this pain and taking up all of your precious time to redo papers that I had in my possession the whole time." I was happy that my grade was increased but still hurt from the lack of feeling. I ended up with a C in the class anyway because of the final, which contained questions from lessons that we had never gone over in class.

(Word count: 509)

5

CAMPUS NARRATIVES, SHORT RESPONSES, AND NON-NARRATIVE RESPONSES

T HE ESSAYS IN THE first four chapters illustrate basic techniques that can be harnessed to write on virtually any subject you choose and to respond to virtually any kind of application prompt. The essays in this chapter harness these techniques, but they do this by meeting an extra condition set by a certain kind of application prompt. The first two essays in this chapter effectively use narrative to put their authors right on the campuses of their desired schools, in response to the kind of prompt that asks broadly "Why our school?" You will find the same principles at work in these two essays as you do in the essays from the previous four chapters. These narrative techniques help the admissions reader imagine the author on campus (see Chapter 9).

The remaining essays are short responses (shorter than roughly three hundred words) that either use narrative to get to the point quickly or that offer direct non-narrative responses to college prompts. Again, short narratives use the techniques illustrated in the essays so far to make quick work of responding to a prompt in an even lower word count. In these essays, narrative provides a foothold and controlled ending for essays that never seem long enough to get a point across.

Finally, you might think of non-narrative responses as lyric responses but without the strong emotional appeal or reflective qualities. Rather, a non-narrative response treats a prompt more directly than a narrative or lyric response does. It might be used to answer a question about potential areas of academic interests or majors, about extenuating personal circumstances, or about low grades—topics that could be more effectively treated in a direct manner. Still, narrative and lyric writing will help you address the majority of your prompts creatively.

Limitless
G. K.

"Sorry, but I can't give you those classes. You know that the school is out of funds, and you're only allowed to have seven periods a day. I am just going to give you what you need. And that is final."

"But I really want those classes, mister…"

"Rules are rules, and your schedule is already full. So I can't really pull any strings here, and let's say that I do give you those classes. The program office is going to change it anyway. So what's the point? Just take what I give you."

"All right, fine, since I have no choice."

Though I said it was fine, I was about to burst into flames declaring how unfair this was. All I ever wanted was to take the classes that I wouldn't normally get the chance to take outside of the school. Before, the school was able to fund kids taking more classes than they needed, but now it limited kids from taking classes that they wanted because of the budget cuts from the City of New York.

As I was listening to the information session at Swarthmore College, I knew immediately that this would be a college that I would like to attend. But what really grabbed my attention was that students, dedicated to what they did, could design their own majors.

The college does not make money a big issue to limit students from doing what they have a passion for; instead they try to find any sort of scholarship or aid to help students achieve their goals. It was then I realized that Swarthmore made it possible for their students to be limitless in what they could do when it came to pursing their dreams.

(Word count: 289)

One Hundred Percent
Amanda Chiodo

"Oh, one moment. Let me just wait until the train passes," shouted the tour guide as she walked backward. After the train rushed by, she resumed talking: "Okay, so down this street is where the School of Hospitality Administration is. Last year they actually had a one-hundred-percent employment rate after graduation." My jaw dropped to the ground as I turned to face my dad, whose face mirrored my own. My whole future flashed before my eyes and it all seemed so tangible.

"One-hundred-percent employment rate right after graduation?" I whispered to my dad as we continued walking. All he could muster up to say was "Wow!" as he remained in total amazement. "That is like practically being guaranteed a job right out of college!" I thought to myself as everything else the tour guide said suddenly faded.

There it was, my future laid out right in front of me. In those few words. She could have forgotten to mention those simple words, and I might have never known. I might have never known that, if I applied to Boston University for a degree in hospitality management, it would not be a struggle for me to obtain a job after graduation. Boston University's hospitality program is just as predominant as any other program in the university, and that is very comforting to someone like me who hopes to succeed in the hospitality industry. One day I hope to be traveling the world or be managing a large stadium or theatre. I know that Boston University will provide me the tools to prosper in the real world and succeed in all those aspirations I hold.

(Word count: 276)

The Joys of Defeat
Chris C.

Tap. Tap. The wrestling match had started only moments before and a winner had already emerged. I rose from the mat victorious, loosening my uncomfortable headgear. I felt unstoppable; I had pinned him in only thirty seconds. I extended my hand to help my opponent up. Then the referee lifted my arm to signify me as the winner. I extended my hand to my opponent once again and mouthed, "Nice match."

The following week, I heard the familiar tapping of the mat by the referee. This time I was on the receiving end of the beating. I was put onto my back in seven seconds flat. It didn't feel nearly as good as winning, but I still arose from the mat and unstrapped my headgear—same as the week before. After the referee had raised my opponent's arm in victory, I reached my hand out to my opponent and told him, "Nice match."

My approach to every match was recognized when, at the end of the season, I was awarded with the sportsmanship award. Although I do not wrestle anymore, I have kept this approach and applied it in my everyday life. It was not something that I have always enjoyed doing: I have wanted to get excited after a big win or angry after a miserable defeat. But my parents played a big role in my approach to winning and losing by being there to put everything in perspective. Now I do it for myself. I have found that whether you win or lose, the only thing that really matters is what you get out of it. So no matter the outcome, after the final tap of the mat, I just get up.

(Word count: 288)

Music, My Salvation
Gabriella Malek

I recently heard a report of a Polish conductor and his collection of rare batons. The report detailed that one of his most poignant pieces was fashioned from wood and bones fished from a soup bowl. The baton had been presented to a music teacher in a WWII concentration camp by his fellow captives. In their darkest hours, these individuals used music to survive unthinkable horrors. Upon hearing the report, my mind immediately fell on my great-grandfather, who had been a conductor in Vienna prior to the war. His prominence in music perhaps saved his family. Even when his luck ran out, he was still able to bring up the spirits of those around him with his music. It was his passion before the war, his savior through it, and his salvation thereafter.

The makeshift baton, which has captured my intrigue, is the physical representation of something that runs deep within me: the transformational quality of music. Though these stories may seem profound, I relate them to everyday life. I find myself transformed at the sound of music. It lifts my mood and energizes me. It makes me reflective and sometimes even melancholy. I feel it coursing through my blood like an electric charge. It keeps me alive as it did for my relatives and those I didn't know during the Holocaust, but with whom I share so much in common.

(Word count: 234)

Cookie Therapy
Carolyn P.

After a track meet I walk into my house. It is 7:00 p.m., and I have hours of homework ahead. The impossibility of the impending evening looms over me, creating an aura of stress that even my usually relaxing shower can't wash off. I plan to work until 9:00 p.m.—until I am overwhelmed by the fact that I will be up through the early hours of the morning. This is when the blissful realization comes. It hits me about once a month as I lean over Spanish worksheets and calculus problems.

There is no way to get this done without being tired tomorrow. So why hurry? I have all night.

I put my pencil down, collect my cool, and walk downstairs. Within half an hour, the batter of my "stress cookies" is made. The first batch heads into the oven, and with it my anxiety seeps away.

It will all get done. The track meet went well and that matters. I like making cookies and that matters too.

I pull out that Spanish worksheet to tackle while the cookies bake. The appropriate balance between complete focus and utter relaxation invigorates me as I tackle the work ahead. Everything always gets done earlier than I expect it to, and I attribute this to karma's way of justifying taking care of myself.

(Word count: 223)

Debate
Carolyn P.

I stood in Foreign Policy Debate with my hands shaking, wondering if this class really belonged in the utopia with which I had become comfortable. At my high school, lab-based science and seminar-style English classes made the core of the collaborative, experiential education to which I had become accustomed. Learning from my peers was part of what I loved about Seattle's Bush School. Yet as I prepared for this day, the one-on-one debate style felt more like a battle of sources, statistics, and quotes than a give and take of ideas. I hated every minute I spent trying to get ahead of my classmates, trying to win. It seemed to me that the caliber of debate could only improve by pooling resources and data.

When the debate began, though, it wasn't the nitty-gritty research that mattered but the logic woven through facts and figures. The research was what my opponent and I stood on, but the intellectual discourse flowed from the reasoning each person presented. In debate, the point was to disagree; thus, both arguments were made stronger through pinpointing their flaws. The politeness that surrounded English discussions, while vital to discussing Life of Pi, got in the way here. So I embraced the class for its subtle form of collaboration.

(Word count: 212)

What Jared Diamond Taught Me
Lauren Beriont

When I first opened the book and began to read, I was overwhelmed by the extreme curiosity of the subject matter that attracted me to Jared Diamond's *Guns, Germs, and Steel*. It was an AP World History assignment; at least, that was all it was supposed to be. As I held it, I could feel that it was more than just pages glued together or ink on recycled trees. It was an instrument that set me on the path to my future. With my legs crossed by the ankles and my sunglasses pressed against my nose, my back formed to the bends of the maple tree in my side yard, I then set out on an adventure with Diamond. Together we were challenged by the ideas that seemed extraneous, challenged by the amount of information we were absorbing. We traveled through jungles, deserts, savannas, islands, mountains, and farmlands. We met the developing civilizations that had shaped our modern world. We fought off armies and watched civilizations fall, watched empires being born.

I decided right there and then that my dream was to answer his inquiries by discovering how civilization evolved into what we know as the modern world. I was completely infatuated with history and captured by the ideas of science. So I would delve into the unquestioned factors that shaped history and prove answers or find solutions using science. I would fulfill my dream of traveling the world, then teaching all I learned. I knew I could never be bored or unsatisfied because not once did those five hundred pages bore me.

We all sat in class, pencils in hand, paper laid before us. I wrote about the strengths and weaknesses of Diamond's argument, creating new theories using the facts presented in the book. It was a challenge to say the least, my hand cramped and covered in graphite, my mind focused and clear about the future.

(Word count: 323)

PART II
TECHNIQUES

What Makes the Personal Essay Tick: A Look at Narrative-Lyric Balance

T HE KEY TO MAKING the most of your essay space is to strike a conscious balance between narrative and lyric modes. Simple definitions of these terms follow:

- **Narrative**—a story; the technique of storytelling.
- **Lyric**—expression of thoughts and feelings.[3]
- **Mode**—manner; how something is done or how it happens.

You can think of the narrative and lyric modes as you would various modes of transportation, or vehicles: they both "get you there" (that is, convey information in your essay), but each with a different feel. For example, if a "narrative" form of exercise is running—simple, straightforward, and efficient—then you might say that a "lyric" form of exercise is something more relaxing or tranquil, like yoga. A narrative film might be a fast-paced action flick, whereas a lyric film could be one of those artsy French films. Narrative communication: Facebook. Lyric communication: snail mail.

The following chart has a Narrative column and a Lyric column. In each column are analogies sorted by themes that are meant to help

---

3. Naturally, most people first think of music when they hear the word *lyric*. As a mode of writing, the word has a related but more specific meaning.

you understand how the two modes can be used to impact the way you write. In the space provided, complete the chart to get a better sense for this difference. There's no single right answer, only those that help you understand this difference.

Narrative	Lyric
creates mood and tone in a story	creates mood and tone in reflection
taking the subway to work	
	dining at a fine restaurant
reading the newspaper	
	owning a pet owl
The *Odyssey*, The *Iliad*	

When you've completed the chart, look at the one that follows for sample responses, along with explanations.

Take a look at the completed chart. Are any of your analogies similar to the examples provided here? Read the explanations that follow for more insight.

Narrative	Lyric
creates mood and tone in a story	creates mood and tone in reflection
taking the subway to work	**taking a detour through Central Park on your way to work in your chauffeured limousine**
grabbing a quick bite to eat in the car	dining at a fine restaurant
reading the newspaper	**reading a romance novel**
owning a pet cat	owning a pet owl
The *Odyssey*, The *Iliad*	**Shakespeare's sonnets**

So what's the difference between the two modes exactly? In the first example, taking the subway to work is a relatively inexpensive, plain mode of transportation. You'd take the most direct line and likely get off at the closest stop to your place of employment. However, taking a chauffeured limousine (implied wealth aside) would suggest a mode of transportation above and beyond the function of getting from one place to another. You could relax in a comfy seat, listen to music on a high-quality sound system, and enjoy the views of the park. You would not be in a particular rush.

In the fourth example, if you wanted to own a pet, getting a cat would be a fairly conventional, direct mode (way) of doing this. You could go to a pet store and buy one, or you could adopt from a friend or a shelter. On the other hand, to obtain a pet owl, you'd likely have to trap it by yourself or come by it in perhaps an illegal manner. Owning an owl would inspire a certain mystique and awe that owning a plain house cat would not.

The point of these analogies is most directly embodied in the last example. The epic poems the *Odyssey* and the *Iliad* are narrative-driven. While they are embellished with descriptions, feelings, and lovely poetic language, they are first and foremost great stories. Shakespeare's sonnets, naturally, have narrative elements too, but his poems are far more admired for their passionate lyric expression than for their stories. Perhaps a play by Shakespeare—say, *Macbeth*—best represents how narrative and lyric modes can work together rapturously: profound, poetic dialogue that nonetheless drives a gripping narrative.

To sum it up, the examples in the Narrative column "get the job done": they fulfill their respective demands directly and with more emphasis on content than on style or feeling. The examples in the Lyric column "take their time": they are more concerned with mood, feeling, and style. They serve their respective functions as well as do the narrative examples, but with an expressive, qualitative difference. Ultimately, a controlled blend of the two modes will constitute your best essays.

Read the following essays. Mark the transitions between narrative and lyric modes using *E1* (first narrative event), *E2* (second narrative event), and *L* (lyric reflection). Also ask yourself what types of prompts this essay could be used to address.

Essay Exercise

December 24th
Kayleigh Kangas

Paragraph 1   I slowly peeled back the cardboard to reveal the chocolate in the Advent calendar. Every time I opened a new door, it was more exciting than the last, and as every child knows, the last chocolate, the chocolate of December 24th, is always Santa. "You know," my mom said as she walked into the kitchen, "when I was a child, Christmas was very different. You see, even though I had six brothers and sisters, there were only three of us still living at home while I was growing up. The others had grown up and moved off to start their own lives, but they always came home for Christmas. We didn't have very much money, and we didn't have a very big Christmas. Every year though, my whole family came to the house, which became almost unbearably crowded and packed with relatives." She walked over to the refrigerator and pulled out the Pepsi, pouring herself a glass. "When I woke up on Christmas morning, I didn't walk out to a living room full of gifts like you do every year. You girls are very fortunate to have such a wonderful Christmas. We got presents, sure, but not like you do. Many times, I unwrapped a sweater or a pair of pants on Christmas morning. That's why I always make sure you girls have a nice Christmas to wake up to." She walked out into the living room, switched on the TV, and sat on the couch. I continued on my merry way with the precious Santa chocolate in hand, not really thinking much about what my mom had said.

Paragraph 2

About a month earlier, we had cut down our Christmas tree. We woke up in the morning, and my parents bundled me up in plenty of warm clothes before we got in the car. On the way to the Christmas tree farm, we put the tape in and sang Christmas carols the whole way there. When we arrived, my dad grabbed a saw off the rack. "Need a lift?" said the man on the tractor with the trailer. We all hopped on the trailer and found a cozy seat on the hay. Once we had found the perfect tree, my dad and sisters cut it down and carried it back to the front of the farm. At home, while my dad prepared the tree and tree stand in the garage, my mom, my sisters, and I were in the kitchen preparing the smorgasbord that we would enjoy while we decorated the tree.

Paragraph 3

Christmas is not about the presents, and although we all know that, I feel like I've been raised to understand it even more so than others. As a child, my mom never had the luxury of thinking that Christmas revolved around presents, and she proved the importance of family to me by raising me with so many Christmas traditions that revolved around family. That story means more to my mother than it does to me, but she carried out the moral of that story in the way she brought me up.

(Word count: 514)

So how would you mark the distribution of the narrative and lyric modes? In the space provided, write *E1* (first narrative event), *E2* (second narrative event), or *L* (lyric reflection) next to each of the paragraph numbers:

Paragraph 1: _____

Paragraph 2: _____

Paragraph 3: _____

And how much of this essay would you say is spent in narrative mode? How much in lyric mode?

Narrative mode: _____ percent of the essay

Lyric mode: _____ percent of the essay

Types of prompts this essay could be used to address: _____

_____

Compare your responses to those that follow.

Answers and Explanations

Paragraph 1: <u>E1</u>

Paragraph 2: <u>E2</u>

Paragraph 3: <u>L</u>

The first paragraph (E1) clearly starts in narrative mode. From the beginning of the essay, the author grounds her writing in a specific moment: "I slowly peeled back the cardboard to reveal the chocolate in the Advent calendar." The rest of the narrative in this first paragraph continues directly from that moment, with virtually no jump in time. Even when dialogue develops with her mother, the author is careful to keep us in the moment still with clever, short actions: "'You know,' my mom *said as she walked into the kitchen,* 'when I was a child, Christmas was very different.'" The italicized description of her mother's actions doesn't seem that important to the story but, in fact, it performs the simple and vital task of keeping the narrative grounded in time and space.

The second paragraph (E2) continues in the narrative mode, as is clear by the descriptions of the family getting up early and venturing out to cut down a Christmas tree. But this narrative action does not take place at the same time or in the same space as does the action in the first paragraph: "*About a month earlier,* we had cut down our Christmas tree," hence, the distinction of E2.

In this essay, lyric reflection (L) appears in the third paragraph, which does not include any narrative elements (that is, nothing happens in it). Rather, the author moves on to reflect on the meaning of Christmas after connecting dots between the two events that turned up in her memory when sitting down to write this essay.

In short, the lyric mode will naturally arise when you have hit on an event or two that you feel are worth writing about. These events can be years or minutes apart, but they are obviously connected in some way.

What these events equal when you add them together is essentially the feelings they bring out in you, captured by your lyric reflection.

In this essay, given that the narrative elements E1 and E2 take up the larger first two paragraphs, respectively, and that the lyric reflection (L) occupies the third paragraph, you could estimate the proportions at about two-thirds to three-fourths narrative and the remainder lyric. Remember, these proportions are not fixed for every essay.

As for the essay topics, this piece could be used to answer common prompts, such as those asking applicants to reflect on important events in their lives, on the influences of others, or on important lessons they've learned. As it stands, this essay addresses all these topics, and it could be modified to address others.

Take another look at lyric-narrative proportion in the following essay and mark the transitions between narrative and lyric modes using *E1* (first narrative event), *E2* (second narrative event), and *L* (lyric reflection). Once again, ask yourself what types of prompts this essay could be used to address.

Essay Exercise

Adella
Carly David

Paragraph 1   I took the picture that my mother had given me delicately in my hands and examined it more closely.

Paragraph 2   It had been flawlessly preserved and had beautiful shades of dark browns and off-whites. The picture was of one solitary girl, nearly my age. She did not have a smile on her face but a solemn expression. An expression that made me think back to times that were much simpler than my own.

Paragraph 3   I grasped the picture lightly on the edges, trying not to leave a smudge mark. My mother leaned over me to get a look at the picture and asked, "Do you know who this is?"

I gave my mom a confused look and shook my head. I had an idea of who it looked like, but I did not want to give the wrong answer. I tenderly flipped over the picture and read the name printed on the back: Adella. I smiled in the realization that the picture was of my great-grandmother.

Paragraph 4   Pictures were a different thing back then. They were a valuable keepsake and a luxury. Teenagers did not have flirty poses or digital cameras to erase any blemish. What a person looked like in reality was what the picture looked like; it was a reflection, not a deception.

Paragraph 5   There was nothing much to the picture. There was a chair in the center of the room. My then-fourteen-year-old great-grandmother leaned slightly onto the chair. She stood a little uncomfortably in a dress that extended from her neck to her ankles.

Paragraph 6   I imagined this photo being taken. She must have been at a house taking a series of family photos. I am sure her twelve brothers and sisters were staring at her as the photographer told her how to position herself. She wanted to just stand in the picture and have it be done with, but the photographer insisted on using a prop. My great-grandmother slowly walked over to the chair that was placed near her. She looked straight into the lens, unafraid. She did not smile because none of her older brothers or sisters had and she wanted to follow suit. She was uncomfortable but managed to keep her eyes from blinking long enough for the photographer to get an exposure. She would have to wait for the picture to be processed before she could say if she had done a good job.

Paragraph 7   I looked down once more at the photo and smiled. Looking intensely into the picture's eyes, I could see the spark of life that my great-grandmother still thrived on. The picture was simple but elegant, static but full of life.

(Word count: 437)

So how would you mark the distribution of the narrative and lyric modes? In the space provided, write *E1* (first narrative event), *E2* (second narrative event), or *L* (lyric reflection) next to each of the paragraph numbers:

Paragraph 1: _____

Paragraph 2: _____

Paragraph 3: _____

Paragraph 4: _____

Paragraph 5: _____

Paragraph 6: _____

Paragraph 7: _____

And how much of this essay would you say is spent in narrative mode? How much in lyric mode?

Narrative mode: _____ percent of the essay

Lyric mode: _____ percent of the essay

Types of prompts this essay could be used to address: _____

_____

Compare your responses to those that follow.

Answers and Explanations

Paragraph 1: <u>E1</u>

Paragraph 2: <u>E1</u>

Paragraph 3: <u>E1</u>

Paragraph 4: <u>L</u>

Paragraph 5: <u>E1</u>

Paragraph 6: <u>E2</u>

Paragraph 7: <u>E1</u>

Although the author of "Adella" breaks her essay into smaller paragraphs than those in the previous essay, they each still fall into the narrative or lyric modes.

Paragraph 1 clearly starts in the moment, necessarily defining the first narrative event (E1). Until the author transitions out of this moment in which she is looking at the photograph, we remain in E1. As such, the second and third paragraphs continue in this moment, with a description of the photograph and conversation between the speaker and her mother.

The fourth paragraph, though, does not contribute to the narrative moment. Rather, the writer has used the established narrative ground as a springboard to reflect on photographs then and now: "it was a reflection, not a deception." Neither part of the established narrative moment or the one to come, this paragraph stands on its own as lyric reflection (L).

Paragraph 5 returns to a description of the photograph, so it most accurately belongs to E1. The sixth paragraph, however, represents something new in the essay: a reimagining of the photography session in that distant era (E2), which builds on the lyric reflection and narrative so far. This paragraph is an act of creativity but also one of imaginative footwork, an attempt to characterize someone in her youth.

The final paragraph, then, transitions back to E1, in which the author brings the effects of the two eras together and ends with a subtle appreciation of her great-grandmother. With regard to narrative-lyric proportion in "Adella," only the fourth paragraph stands out as explicitly lyric, so of the seven small paragraphs, it represents about one-fifth of the essay. So this essay is, again, largely narrative; you can see, however, how the structure and mix of the two modes in "Adella" differ from that of "December 24th."

The content of this personal essay lends itself to answering prompts about an important photograph, an important realization, or another such prompt that asks the applicant to describe family or a moment of personal understanding. Whatever the prompt this essay was written to answer, the applicant clearly demonstrates narrative-lyric control, solid writing skills, and sensitivity.

Essay Exercise

Gospel
Robbie Trocchia

Paragraph 1   "Amen." The church vibrates with voices in robotic unison, followed by the loud creaking of wooden pews as people take their seats. This Sunday morning is consumed by my family's weekly tradition of attending Mass, something that my siblings and I have always dreaded. But the hour of thoughtful reflection that this despised routine provides is more than just an opportunity to let my mind wander. It has given me the chance to think about why I'm kneeling with my hands crossed at my chest when I'd rather be somewhere else.

Paragraph 2   Church has always been a part of my family's way of life. We attend Mass every week (except for days when my younger brother has a Pop Warner game), and on Christmas and Easter. My church offers a comfortable environment in which my family can enjoy the stable and obliging community that it comprises. However, over the past few years, as I have continued to absorb everything that passes my eyes, I have come to personal conclusions and I have developed personal convictions.

Paragraph 3   In response to the Church's views on marriage, I simply do not understand the sovereignty of what lies in people's pants over what lies in their hearts. And I just don't get why a man is preaching to me, knowing that a woman is prohibited from standing in his place. I could continue with a tirade against the Church, but I have come to realize what a waste of time that would be. What is important is that I have come to understand the dilemma that I am facing, the struggle between falsely sharing in my family's contentment while I come to realize that my personal ideals do not align with those of my supposed faith. Although my religious upbringing has always felt natural to me, my own beliefs hold more worth for who I am, despite the familial ties I have to the Church.

Paragraph 4   This weekly tradition represents something that is different for every person in my family. While it may provide someone else with the chance to speak to God, it has allowed me to think about my personal needs in regard to spirituality and peace of self. I have come to find that the faith I was brought up in does not provide me with satisfaction, and I have indeed articulated my discontent to my family; however, I cannot help but feel guilt as I turn my back on my family's beliefs, accompanied by a sharp sense of isolation in what I stand for. It feels as if I am torn between my family and myself, and the notion of pursuing my best interests sounds selfish and hurtful. But what is best for me?

My simplest response would be happiness, and at this point in my life, I am uncertain as to whether religion can guide me toward that happiness. Perhaps I will need it in the future, as my mom insists; however, reflecting quietly in a church will have to do for now. Instead, I can gaze around the church, pondering endlessly, feeling at ease knowing that being there for my family is what really counts. Amen.

(Word count: 526)

So how would you mark the distribution of the narrative and lyric modes? In the space provided, write *E1* (first narrative event), *E2* (second narrative event), or *L* (lyric reflection) next to each of the paragraph numbers:

Paragraph 1: _____

Paragraph 2: _____

Paragraph 3: _____

Paragraph 4: _____

And how much of this essay would you say is spent in narrative mode? How much in lyric mode?

Narrative mode: _____ percent of the essay

Lyric mode: _____ percent of the essay

Types of prompts this essay could be used to address: _____

_____

Compare your responses to those that follow.

Answers and Explanations

Paragraph 1: <u>E1</u>

Paragraph 2: <u>L</u>

Paragraph 3: <u>L</u>

Paragraph 4: <u>L/E1</u>

The first paragraph of "Gospel" starts in the narrative mode, since we are given a description of the church setting and of the parishioners' actions in the moment, in the present tense. In keeping with the nature of memory, this key narrative chunk quickly gives rise to lyric reflection in the subsequent paragraphs. The transition that sets this up comes at the end of the first paragraph: "It has given me the chance to think about why I'm kneeling with my hands crossed at my chest when I'd rather be somewhere else."

The paragraphs that follow delve into this *why*, and we spend time in this lyric state until the end of the final paragraph: "however, *reflecting quietly in a church will have to do for now.* Instead, I can gaze around the church, pondering endlessly, feeling at ease knowing that being there for my family is what really counts. Amen." The part italicized here emphasizes that the essay has indeed returned briefly to the narrative mode, to wrap things up. The author provides a subtle symmetry by finishing with the same key word with which he starts; *amen*, though, has become infused with a new, personal meaning that allows him to reconcile his personal opinions with the desire to spend time with his family.

As such, of the four paragraphs that constitute "Gospel," one and a half of them occupy the narrative mode, for about 40 percent of the essay. Slightly more favor is given to the lyric mode, and this fills in the middle of the essay, while the narrative mode bookends the reflections.

Finally, potential prompts that this essay could be used to address might include something that asks about an important decision you've had to make in your life, a family tradition or ritual, a challenge you've faced growing up, a personal truth you've come to, or a way in which you have changed.

Remember that essays do not need to "answer" prompts directly so much as they should associatively. Keeping this sense of restriction at bay will allow you more creative license in writing your essays and may even allow you to use an essay for two or more college prompts, with minor modifications.

Essay Exercise

Balance
Claire Perry

Paragraph 1

I clamp my tired hand around the cool glass doorknob whose ridges fit perfectly in my palm. After twelve years, we are old friends. Every morning, we shake hands and he wishes me well on my way to school. With a simple twist and a little help from the wind, the heavy door swings back for me and we begin our dance. Going backward and carefully maneuvering, first my backpack, then my two pieces of toast, we are caught in the most intricate of tangos. My most recent art project flails about, and I desperately try not to spill my beloved cup of tea.

Paragraph 2

"BYE, MOM! BYE, DAD! BYE, CARY!" I bellow up the stairs. I do not expect a response. My family is still asleep, having yet to begin pressing their snooze buttons.

Paragraph 3

I step out into the gray morning. The wet cement sidewalk sends a wave of chills up my spine; my bare feet are not expecting the rain from last night to have left so much of its nip behind. I take some bites of my toast; I always eat while walking to school. "Efficiency," I say whenever someone asks.

Paragraph 4   The wind plays with my hair, and the trees dance around. A few lonely cars whiz by. The few drivers to pass me crane their necks back and slow down, flaunting baffled expressions. I am not sure if this is due to my balancing act, lack of shoes, or just because of the time. Whatever the reason they stare, I don't mind.

Paragraph 5   I grip my tea more tightly. Today I am not in a rush—no club meeting, no urgent need to see my teachers—just going in to sit with my friends in the hallway. The weight of my backpack grows heavier, but as I cross the unassuming one-way street, the high school comes into view. No more cold cement, now my feet carry me across the dew-covered pitch. The Canadian geese give me dirty looks as I trek gingerly across their turf. Begrudgingly, they move out of my way, much more slowly than the seagulls that would reside here in the spring.

Paragraph 6   Up a hill and across the senior parking lot. Few cars are settled in their spots. White Volvo: Kristine is here. So are Pat and Steven. I survey the area for more cars, but no one else has arrived. Cameron, Jenn, and Brittney will be here soon. My friends frequently offer me rides—they pass my house anyway, they say—but I usually decline. They are an important part of my life, but so is the brief solitude of my walks and the balance they bring me.

Paragraph 7   Twelve familiar years of walking to school have anchored me; now they give me leave to explore anew.

(Word count: 463)

So how would you mark the distribution of the narrative and lyric modes? In the space provided, write *E1* (first narrative event), *E2* (second narrative event), or *L* (lyric reflection) next to each of the paragraph numbers:

Paragraph 1: _____

Paragraph 2: _____

Paragraph 3: _____

Paragraph 4: _____

Paragraph 5: _____

Paragraph 6: _____

Paragraph 7: _____

And how much of this essay would you say is spent in narrative mode? How much in lyric mode?

Narrative mode: _____ percent of the essay

Lyric mode: _____ percent of the essay

Types of prompts this essay could be used to address: _____

_____

Compare your responses to those that follow.

Answers and Explanations

Paragraph 1: <u>E1</u>

Paragraph 2: <u>E1</u>

Paragraph 3: <u>E1</u>

Paragraph 4: <u>E1</u>

Paragraph 5: <u>E1</u>

Paragraph 6: <u>E1/L</u>

Paragraph 7: <u>L</u>

"Balance" starts with a simple action—the narrator reaches for the doorknob—and continues in the same narrative moment until the second half of paragraph 6, where a brief lyric suspension ends it. From the initial moment in which the narrative action is established, the author provides a description about her unassuming, routine walk to school.

The author establishes her voice and the key appeal of this essay in her rich attention to the mundane details. It is a narrative essay—there is action and dialogue throughout—but nothing happens. That is, "Balance" presents a subject matter that could be dull if it weren't for the author's awareness of her everyday life and the role that details play in her personal growth. In this slow-moving narrative, she chooses qualitative richness over flashy action. From the cool touch of the doorknob to the spiteful geese, this narrative details the routine that the young woman has developed in making sense of her world. Her attention to detail aside, she is clearly connected with her surroundings, counting good friends. In her recognition of the importance of solitude, she nods to the reader that she has made the most of her high school years. The quiet confidence that she shows in detailing her old surroundings signals that this young woman is indeed ready to venture out for college on her own capable terms.

In reading "Balance," remember that you do not need to justify your content in a personal essay. Rather, a subtle and well-written personal essay will let the reader make the connections or associations between the essay and the prompt on his or her own. This leaves you free to tell a great story and to provide meaningful reflection. Finally, "Balance" could answer a prompt about an important event, routine, or ritual; about your hometown; or about how you have prepared for college. It consists of about 90 percent narrative and 10 percent lyric.

Essay Exercise

On Receiving a Gift from a 445-Year-Old Dead Man
Jennifer Lapp

Paragraph 1

As soon as I held the essay booklet in my hand, AP English Literature and Composition transformed from a class of books and discussions to a tangible test, a labyrinth of words that loved tricks more than successes. Though I had finished the impossible multiple-choice section, I was nervous for the essays. I had no idea what the test would throw at me: which question, which passage, and, more frighteningly, which poem. Despite the nerves, I was calmed by trust. I trusted my books and I especially trusted my arsenal of fictional characters. I knew that Mr. Darcy and Elizabeth Bennet or Romeo and Juliet could guide me to an essay about complex character relationships (Mr. Darcy and Lizzy post-marriage, Romeo and Juliet post-death). A fratricidal Richard III was poised for a villainy question, though I knew I could also steal Mr. Wickham away from seducing yet *another* person's younger sister long enough to help me. For symbolism, Winston would serve me obsequiously, though the poor thing would do so holding his paper weight in front of the painting of St. Clement's Church. If I got a question about fate and free will, Billy Pilgrim would teleport in. My characters and I were ready for anything; no essay could beat us. But when it came to poetry, I was alone. All that my characters could do was wish me luck.

Paragraph 2   If my characters were to stand beside me, William Shakespeare would sit next to me, hold my free hand, and guide me. I relish reading Shakespeare. I was hooked after reading *Romeo and Juliet* and *A Midsummer Night's Dream* in eighth grade. By ninth grade, I viewed my trip to London as would a pilgrim his journey to Mecca. When I first saw the Globe from a boat on the River Thames, it struck me as a visual anomaly; its plaster-and-wood exterior and thatched roof were physically dwarfed by the modernity that surrounded it. Figuratively, however, the Globe surpassed its surroundings by the sheer amount of history crammed inside its "wooden O." Though it wasn't the original struc- ture, it was still a perfect model of the theatre in which Shakespeare's works originally captivated audiences. When I toured inside, I felt Shakespeare beside me as I "treaded the boards" in the cathedral of my obsession.

Paragraph 3   Shakespeare also stood beside me in the most magical moment of my life when I looked down at the poetry prompt. Let's face it, no one expects to find magic during an AP exam, but I did. Shock gripped me as I read the instructions: "Read the following passage from William Shakespeare's *Henry VIII…*" I mentally fell out my chair; I could have cried. There it was. On paper. Proof: Shakespeare loved me. Not only was he there to hold my hand, but he had gone out of his way to help me on the exam.

Paragraph 4   In that magical moment, I realized that literature mattered to me most. It was my teacher. It contained some of
my greatest friends and favorite people in the whole world.
It was my escape from reality. And in that moment, it was
the ultimate confidence booster. On the AP exam, the utter
reassurance sent care of William Shakespeare showed me
my extreme faith and trust in words.

(Word count: 556)

So how would you mark the distribution of the narrative and lyric modes?
In the space provided, write *E1* (first narrative event), *E2* (second narrative event), or *L* (lyric reflection) next to each of the paragraph numbers:

Paragraph 1: _____

Paragraph 2: _____

Paragraph 3: _____

Paragraph 4: _____

And how much of this essay would you say is spent in narrative mode?
How much in lyric mode?

Narrative mode: _____ percent of the essay

Lyric mode: _____ percent of the essay

Types of prompts this essay could be used to address: _____

_____

Compare your responses to those that follow.

Answers and Explanations

Paragraph 1: <u>E1</u>

Paragraph 2: <u>L/E2</u>

Paragraph 3: <u>E1</u>

Paragraph 4: <u>L</u>

The author does a solid job of rooting her narrative in the moment off the bat: "As soon as I held the essay booklet in my hand, AP English Literature and Composition transformed from a class of books and discussions to a tangible test." In the first paragraph, the author continues on to catalogue characters she admires, but with the understanding that she is sitting at the AP test, so the entire first paragraph is anchored in the narrative mode.

The first few lines of the second paragraph are dedicated to the author's love of Shakespeare. The paragraph quickly turns to the moment of the author's trip to England, two years before. The reader follows her into the Globe.

That brief narrative interlude transitions nicely back to the AP exam at hand. As the author admits, she does not expect to find magic on the AP test, but for her, the enchanting course that Shakespeare has followed in her life rewarded her for her devotion on the exam. Because we are in this instant, reading the instructions on the exam with the author, we are clearly back in the first narrative moment.

The author wraps up her essay with a lovely tribute to Shakespeare and literature at large, which she has achieved by intertwining the two narrative moments—magically, in her eyes.

As for narrative-lyric balance, this essays jumps in a controlled manner between the two. The narrative bits are laced with reflections on the importance of Shakespeare and literature in the author's life, and the proportion of each in the essay is about 50 percent.

Potential application prompts that this essay could answer: describe an unexpected surprise; describe a passion of yours; write about a person who is important to you; write about an important moment in your life.

The following chart provides a quick glimpse at how varied the five previous essays alone are in their use of narrative-lyric balance. As you move forward with drafting and revising your own essays, let this breakdown reassure you that there is not just one way to go about this method. Instead, the "right" narrative-lyric balance is going to vary by author, essay, subject, and desired effect. An honest and personal approach to your chosen content will distinguish your essay further.

Essay title	No. of paragraphs	Narrative-Lyric order	Approximate narrative/lyric proportion
"December 24th"	3	E1-E2-L	65/35
"Adella"	7	E1-L-E1-E2-E1	80/20
"Gospel"	4	E1-L-E1	40/60
"Balance"	7	E1-L	90/10
"On Receiving a Gift from a 445-Year-Old Dead Man"	4	E1-L-E2-E1-L	50/50

Not Just Another English Essay: Making Space for Creativity in Personal Writing

THE GUIDELINES IN THIS chapter demonstrate that what makes a good *academic* essay doesn't necessarily make a good *personal* essay. Think about the essays you've read in this book so far and how they open with action, dialogue, or widening lyric reflection. They cover a lot of ground in a short space this way and invite the reader in. Now imagine for a moment using the common American format for establishing an academic argument. If you wrote about personal experiences in an academic structure, it might look something like this:

My older brother is a very important person in my life. Ever since I was a little kid, he has been there for me and has taught me important lessons. There are three experiences that I will never forget: the time he stood up for me against a bully, the time he helped me pass my math class, and the time he took my side in a big argument with my parents.

I've exaggerated the language here to be drab, but that's kind of the point. The "author" opens with a direct answer to an imaginary prompt—let's say, *Tell us about someone who is important to you and why.* The student makes a clear gesture to do this, but in a way that stifles any chance at narrative, at widening lyric reflection, and at using the same personal essay for more than one college. Instead, there is a direct *answer* to the prompt, one that sets up a main idea—thesis—followed by supporting details. We could imagine one body paragraph devoted to each of these supporting details—the bully, math class, and parents. In that case, there would be no sense of surprise or discovery, and the language would remain flat as a result. Narrative would lose out.

Listed below are some common traits of a good academic essay and explanations of why these traits can stifle your personal essay. By following these guidelines, you'll maximize the creative possibilities of your personal narrative and develop a single essay to use or modify for several colleges' essay prompts. What's more, you'll cover more ground—reveal more about yourself—in narrative and lyric modes while keeping your reader entertained. The essays that follow are real students' drafts with comments meant to open their essays to narrative and lyric modes.

Breaking the Rules of Academic Writing

First, high school students are usually told not to use the first person in academic writing (which will change in college, by the way). In the personal essay, your *I* is essential.

Thesis

In the personal essay, you do not need to qualify your reasons for writing about one thing or the other; self-conscious commentary is the personal-essay equivalent of the thesis statement in an academic paper—justification for writing about the subject you choose. You shouldn't worry about "answering" the application prompt—not directly, that is. Rather, you can respond to it starting with dialogue or action. Doing so will let the essay take on a life of its own in narrative form.

Commentary

Instead of lyric reflection—which should create space for the reader to insert her- or himself into the text—self-conscious commentary blocks the reader from further interpretation by pointing out the value or meaning of an event, person, place, or other object of reflection. Examples of self-conscious commentary include *That's when I knew my life would never be the same; My mother is the most important person to me, and I will always be there for her; This photo always puts a smile on my face and reminds me that even a bad event can turn out for the better.* Not only do these self-conscious declarations not leave room for the reader, they do not leave room for meaningful reflection and language—they are flat thoughts flatly expressed. Commentary belongs to neither the narrative nor lyric mode, neither advancing the story nor deepening the reflection.

Take a look at early drafts in progress of three essays you just read in the previous chapter, "Gospel," "Balance," and "On Receiving a Gift from a 445-Year-Old Dead Man." Each draft has original feedback included to help illustrate the workings of the drafting process for these students. After you read the drafts of one essay, reread the final draft to gauge improvements over the course of the drafting process.

Gospel
Robbie Trocchia

"Amen." The church vibrates with voices in robotic unison, followed by the loud creaking of wooden pews as people take their seats. This Sunday morning, ~~like almost every other Sunday morning of my existence,~~ is consumed by my family's weekly tradition of attending Mass, something that my siblings and I have always dreaded. But the hour of thoughtful reflection that this despised routine provides is more than just an opportunity to let my mind wander. It has given me the chance to think about why I'm kneeling with my hands crossed at my chest when I'd rather be somewhere else.

Church has always been a part of my

> Implied by "weekly" below.

family's way of life. We attend Mass every week (except for days when my younger brother has a Pop Warner game), and on Christmas and Easter. My church offers a comfortable environment in which my family can enjoy the stable and obliging community that it comprises. However, over the past few years, as I have continued to absorb everything that passes my eyes, I have come to personal conclusions and I have developed personal convictions.

In response to the Church's views on marriage, I simply do not understand the sovereignty of what lies in people's pants over what lies in their hearts. And I just don't get why a man is preaching to me, knowing that a woman is prohibited from standing in his place. I could continue with a tirade against the Church, but I have come to realize what a waste of time that would be. What is important is that I have come to understand the dilemma that I am facing, the struggle between falsely sharing in my family's contentment while I come to realize that my personal ideals do not align with those of my supposed faith. Although my religious upbringing has always felt natural to me, my own beliefs hold more worth for who I am, despite the familial ties I have to the Church.

This weekly tradition represents something that is different for every person in my family. While it may provide someone else with the chance to speak to God, it has allowed me to think about my personal needs in regard to spirituality and peace of self. I have come to find that the faith I was brought up in does not provide me with satisfaction, and I have indeed articulated my discontent to my family; however, I cannot help but feel guilt as I turn my back on my family's beliefs, accompanied by a sharp sense of isolation in what I stand for. It feels as if I am torn between my family and myself, and the notion of pursuing my best interests sounds selfish and hurtful. But what is best for me? My simplest response would be happiness and, at this point in my life, I am uncertain as to whether religion can guide me toward that happiness. Perhaps I will need it in the future, as my mom insists; however, at the present moment, ~~I am content in~~ reflecting quietly in a church will have to do for now.

[Although I am essentially walking away from my religion in a spiritual sense, I do not intend to disengage myself from the weekly tradition. It ~~just~~ does not feel right to stay home alone as my family sits together in a pew, feeling the subtle pleasure in knowing that we are all there together.] Instead, I can gaze around the church, pondering endlessly, feeling at ease knowing that being there for my family is what really counts. [Amen]

~~Although I would like to find solace in the faith that my family shares, I have come to the difficult conclusion that it is not the place for me. But I am not ungrateful for my religious upbringing~~

Word count now is at 582. Should that be too long still, I suggest deleting these four lines, which will bring you to 524. If that is still too long, you could do away with the following two lines, which would bring you to 502.

This is a fine ending, and you have gotten here more concisely and directly than in the previous draft. This more direct route to some sort of short-lived balance and focus on time with your family grounds your essay more. Before, it felt less directed, in my opinion; here, I think you have found a nice balance between rejecting and accepting. Well done.

~~nor the moral predicament that it has
created. It has shown me what it means
to mold my own beliefs and stand by
them, even when they are in opposition to the beliefs and values of my
own family. Although I am essentially
walking away from my religion in a
spiritual sense, I do not intend to disengage myself from the weekly tradition. It just does not feel right to stay
home alone as my family sits together
in a pew, feeling the subtle pleasure in
knowing that we are all there together.
Instead, I can gaze around the church,
pondering endlessly; feeling at ease
knowing that being there for my
family is what really counts. Amen.~~

"Gospel" starts out with a well-established narrative ground and central scene on which to build in later drafts: the speaker is look-ing around his church during prayer, which gives rise to the personal insights that follow. Even if word count were not an issue, the final paragraph in the first draft presented here overshoots a subtle closing that brings the essay full circle: "Amen."

The first word of the essay—*amen*—establishes the narrative ground because the speaker is pronouncing it in the moment, but it is also the "Amen" of the Church that the speaker next tries to come to personal grips with.

This last paragraph gets cut in the final draft:

Although I would like to find solace in the faith that my family shares, I have come to the difficult conclusion that it is not the place for me. But I am not ungrateful for my religious upbringing nor the moral predicament that it has created. It has shown me what it means to mold my own beliefs and stand by them, even when they are in opposition to the beliefs and values of my own family. Although I am essentially walking away from my religion in a spiritual sense, I do not intend to disengage myself from the weekly tradition. It just does not feel right to stay home alone as my family sits together in a pew, feeling the subtle pleasure in knowing that we are all there together. Instead, I can gaze around the church, pondering endlessly; feeling at ease knowing that being there for my family is what really counts. Amen.

It's not a bad paragraph, and again, there is a gesture here that winds down the essay nicely. Strangely, the author seems to have repeated himself in the final two paragraphs of the first draft (he told me how late he was up finishing the essay, so it could just be an issue of fatigue), a fact that lends itself to some easily made cuts for length and content.

Now reread the final draft of this essay in Chapter 6. The key to the success of the final draft of this essay—aside from its mature and sober assessment of some big issues—is the personal *amen* on which the essay ends. The author's subtle and effective use of that word says a lot more than the many other words that have been deleted before it. By getting rid of some of the repetitious, understood commentaries toward the end of the first draft, the writer succeeds in arriving at the punctuation of his message in one hundred fewer words than before. And he ditches the academic need to provide justification for his choice of topic and supporting details.

As you will see time and again in impactful personal essays, this kind of subtle ending allows the reader to interpret *amen* in a more engaged and interested way than would be possible with its value assigned by commentary. When college admissions are in the balance, you want the ending of your essay to incite a conversation with the reader. To my mind, the best way to do this is to leave your reader the space to insert him-/herself at the end.

Title idea?—Steps/A Walk/ The Walk to School/Balance
Claire Perry

I clamp my tired hand around the cool glass doorknob, whose ridges fit perfectly in my palm. After twelve years, we are old friends. Every morning, we shake hands and he wishes me well on my way to school. With a simple twist and a little help from the ~~raging~~ wind, the heavy door swings back for me and we begin our dance. Going backward and carefully maneuvering, first my backpack, then my two pieces of toast, we are caught in the most intricate of tangos. My ~~most recent~~ art project flails about, and I desperately try not to spill my beloved cup of tea.

"BYE, MOM! BYE, DAD! BYE, CARY!" I bellow up the stairs. I do not expect a response. My family is still asleep, having yet to begin pressing their snooze buttons.

I step out into the gray morning. The wet cement sidewalk sends a wave of chills up my spine; my bare feet are not expecting the rain from last night to have left so much of its nip behind. I take some bites of my toast; I always eat while walking to school. "Efficiency," I say whenever someone asks. ~~me about it.~~

The wind plays with my hair, and the trees dance around. A few lonely cars whiz by. The few drivers to pass me crane their necks back and slow down, flaunting baffled expressions. I am not sure if this is due to my balancing

> Just suggestions. The title doesn't have to be fancy.

act, lack of shoes, or just because of the time. Whatever the reason they stare, I don't mind.

I grip my tea more tightly. Today I am not in a rush—no club meeting, no urgent need to see my teachers—just going in to sit with my friends in the hallway. The weight of my backpack grows heavier, but as I cross the unassuming one-way street, the high school comes into view. No more cold cement, now my feet carry me across the dew-covered pitch. The Canadian geese give me dirty looks as I trek gingerly across their turf. Begrudgingly, they move out of my way, much more slowly than the seagulls that [would] reside here in the spring.

> Keeps tense.

Up a hill and across the senior parking lot. Few cars are settled in their spots. White Volvo: Kristine is here. So are Pat and Steven. I survey the area for more cars, but no one else has arrived. Cameron, Jenn, and Brittney will be here soon. My friends frequently offer me rides—they pass my house anyway, they say—but I usually decline. They are an important part of [my] life, but so is the brief solitude of my walks; ~~it's about balance.~~ <u>and the balance they bring me.</u>

> Mention of friends and your sense of requiring balance hardly make you sound like a loner. Still, like you said, you cannot help others' interpretations. Just write honestly.

~~My walks have always been an integral part of my life. The destination is never permanent; first elementary school when walks were slow, lyrical, and filled with unconditional love and an outstretched hand to my grandmother. Then, a further~~

~~distance, more independence, and a new sense for friendships as middle school came and went. Usually very gregarious, surrounded by people and engaged in "doing," my walks offer a time to step back and notice and just "be." Usually very observant and understanding of people, my walks offer a time to step back and notice and embrace my surroundings. I will be leaving behind my geese and frozen grass looking forward to another destination - very much~~ grounded ~~in who I am as an individual and very trusting of myself to take the next step.~~

> This doesn't really add anything to your previous remarks. I say, have the confidence to end on a summative note—the line about balance works well. Your reader will also appreciate your directness and brevity.

Take a moment to reread the final draft of this essay in Chapter 6. Similar to the first draft of the preceding essay, "Gospel," from the start of the drafting process, the narrative ground of the essay that would become "Balance" was well established in the writer's eyes. As we communicated about the early drafts, only the lyric portion seemed to be out of alignment with the potential offered by the narrative. It is a narrative that takes time to work itself out but stays controlled and centered on a short and simple event: the walk to school. The soft, gradual nature of the narrative sets the stage for the lyric reflection that the writer thinks should follow.

In the earlier draft, I suggested to the student to completely cut out and rework the final paragraph of the essay:

My walks have always been an integral part of my life. The destination is never permanent; first elementary school when walks were slow, lyrical, and filled with unconditional love and an outstretched hand to my grandmother. Then, a further distance, more independence, and a new sense for friendships as middle school came and went. Usually very gregarious, surrounded by people and engaged in "doing," my walks offer a time to step back and notice and just "be." Usually very observant and understanding of people, my walks offer a time to step back and notice and embrace my surroundings. I will be leaving behind my geese and frozen grass looking forward to another destination—very much grounded in who I am as an individual and very trusting of myself to take the next step.

There is a gesture here that speaks to the mood and tone established in the narrative, but the narrative is cut into incoherent bits that neither extend the narrative moment nor deepen its meaning with lyric reflection. Instead, a statement like "My walks have always been an integral part of my life" overstates the significance of the walks without allowing the reader the enjoyment of coming to this conclusion. A piece of commentary of this sort is what a reader might say in response to a deepening, poetic portion of lyric reflection, in an effort to make sense of the reading. In this first draft, the author blocks that kind of response because she is still in the academic mode of justifying her choice of subject matter. After all, we must figure that walking is important to her on some deep level if she decided to write about it in a college application essay.

In the final draft of "Balance," the author has found a way to extend the narrative in the moment, while bringing it to completion in a simple way that does not bar the reader from making sense of the essay on his or her own: "They are an important part of my life, but so is the brief solitude of my walks and the balance they bring me. Twelve familiar years of walking to school have anchored me; now they give me leave to explore anew."

Especially for an admissions reader, this sort of carefully calibrated open ending gives pause to consider what "explore anew" means to the decision he or she must now make about the fate of this applicant: All things being equal, is this someone we want on our campus?[4] In the

---

4. Not only did this student receive multiple admissions offers from her top college prospects, but one institution asked her permission to use this essay for recruiting purposes, naming it one of the top essays for that application year.

end, the student found balance in replacing her commentary with a soft narrative landing lyrically expressed.

Title?

As soon as I held the essay booklet in my hand, AP English Literature and Composition transformed from ~~the~~ a class of books and discussions to a ~~real and~~ tangible test~~.~~, ~~It was~~ a labyrinth of words ~~which~~ that loved tricks more than successes. Though I had finished the impossible ~~AP English~~ multiple-choice section, I was nervous for the essays. I had no idea what the test would throw at me: which question, which passage, and, more frighteningly, which poem. Despite the nerves, I was calmed by trust. I trusted my books and I especially trusted my characters. I knew that ~~either .~~ Mr. Darcy and Elizabeth Bennet or Romeo and Juliet could ~~guide~~ help me ~~with~~ to an essay about complex character relationships (Mr. Darcy and Lizzy ~~would be~~ post-marriage~~,~~, ~~and~~ Romeo and Juliet ~~would be~~ post-death). A fratricidal Richard III was poised for a villainy question, though I knew I could also steal Mr. Wickham away from seducing yet *another* person's younger sister long enough to ~~be helpful~~ help me. For symbolism, Winston would ~~be able to~~ give me some ideas, though the poor thing would do so ~~as he held~~ holding his ~~glass~~ paper weight ~~and stood~~ in front of the painting of

> Good—you start in the moment.

> serve me obsequiously?

St. Clement's Church. If I got a question about fate ~~versus~~ and free will, Billy Pilgrim would ~~give me tips, though, knowing him, he would probably become unstuck in time at~~ teleport in ~~some point~~. My characters and I were ready for anything; ~~there was~~ no ~~open-ended or passage~~ essay ~~that~~ could beat us. But when it came to poetry, I was alone. All that my characters could do ~~there~~ was ~~smile at me and hope for the best.~~ wish me luck.

~~And so, I held the test in my hand. I opened it [and] looked down at the poetry [prompt].~~

> Insignificant details/Get right to the action.

> You look down again below.

~~Before the magic of the poetry section can be told, my relationship with William Shakespeare must be explained.~~ If my characters were to ~~the~~ stand beside me ~~side~~, William Shakespeare would sit next to me, hold my free hand, and guide me. I relish reading Shakespeare. I was hooked after reading *Romeo and Juliet* and *A Midsummer Night's Dream* in ~~8th~~ eighth grade. By ~~9th~~ ninth grade, I ~~saw~~ viewed my trip to London ~~and the Globe Theatre nearly the same~~ as would a ~~s a~~ pilgrim ~~his~~'s journey to Mecca. When I first saw the Globe ~~for the first time~~ from a boat on the River Thames, it struck me as a visual anomaly,~~;~~ its plaster- and wood~~en~~ exterior ~~and thatched roof were~~ physically dwarfed by the ~~modernity that surrounded it~~ surrounding structures. Figuratively, however, the [Globe] surpassed its

> I think this is a perfectly natural transition. It also keeps the narrative moving smoothly.

> You are fundamentally right in this statement about historical importance, but you do know this is not the original Globe, right?

surroundings by the sheer amount of history crammed inside its ~~famous~~ "wooden O." ~~tetradecagon structure.~~ When I toured ~~the~~ inside, I felt ~~like~~ Shakespeare ~~was~~ beside me as I ~~literally~~ "treaded the boards" ~~of~~ in ~~the theatre that served as~~ the cathedral of my obsession.

~~I think I should also explain that I'm 18 years old and I still believe in magic and William Shakespeare was with me during the most magical moment of my life.~~ Shakespeare strode beside me then, in the most magical moment of my life, and ~~I was given evidence of magic's existence~~ he cemented my belief in magic when I looked down at the poetry prompt. Let's face it, no one expects to find magic during an AP exam, but I did. Shock gripped me as I ~~looked down and~~ read ~~something along the lines of~~ the instructions: "Read the following passage from William Shakespeare's *Henry VIII*..." ~~My heart missed a beat~~ ~~and~~ I mentally fell out my chair; I could have cried. There it was. On paper. Proof~~:~~ Shakespeare loved me. Not only was he there to hold my hand, but he ~~seemed to have~~ had gone out of his way to help me ~~succeed~~ on the exam.

~~From~~ In ~~my~~ that magical ~~experience~~ moment, I realized ~~what~~ that literature mattered ~~is most important~~ to me most. ~~literature.~~ It was~~'s~~ my teacher. It contained~~s~~ some of my greatest friends and favorite people

> Why not use Hamlet's words?

> This, if you ask me, doesn't add anything new to your essay.

> While descriptive, this is cliché. Get right to the fresher image of falling out of your chair mentally—and get on with the essay.

in the whole world. It ~~was~~'s my escape from reality. And, in that moment, it was the ultimate confidence booster. ~~In that moment of my~~ On the AP exam, the utter reassurance sent ~~by~~ care of William Shakespeare showed me my extreme faith and trust in ~~literature~~ words.

~~That trust will never break ever since it proved itself to me so loyally. My esteem for literature plays out across my life: I instinctively respect well-read people; my dream job would be to write books and create characters that inspire people as the characters of Jane Austen, Stephenie Meyer, and William Shakespeare (too name a few) have inspired me.~~ ◄

> Maybe not the same thing, but I thought the shorter word made for a more impactful ending.

> I'd end it right here. The shorter, more abrupt ending will make your reader sorry it's over, instead of making him wish it had stopped sooner.

> Jenn, this looks good. I am glad to see that you have made such good use of the narrative strategies we discussed.

Like "Gospel" and "Balance," "On Receiving a Gift from a 445-Year-Old Dead Man" has a well-established narrative ground—a moment during an important exam—which makes this essay another good candidate for focusing on shifting from commentary to the lyric mode.

Unlike the previous two essays, this one does not suffer from an ending that has overstated the essay's value, nor has it overshot a subtle soft landing in a previous paragraph. Rather, the early draft of "On Receiving a Gift from a 445-Year-Old Dead Man" can benefit from some scalpel cuts around bits of commentary here and there.

For instance, between the first and second large paragraphs comes this transition: "And so, I held the test in my hand. I opened it and looked down at the poetry prompt. Before the magic of the poetry section can be told, my relationship with William Shakespeare must be explained." That notion of *having to* explain the importance of Shakespeare to her is precisely the type of flat justification a writer does not have to include in a personal essay—that's the stuff of academic writing. Instead, the importance of Shakespeare—or soccer or your parents or your religion—will become more apparent to the reader through effective narration and lyric reflection. Even though the writer means to speak lightly about her love of Shakespeare, the justifying commentary delays the natural transition just waiting to be used in the very next sentence: "If my characters were to stand beside me, William Shakespeare would sit next to me, hold my free hand, and guide me." Not only does this sentence set up the second narrative moment of the essay (E2)—the speaker's "pilgrimage" to the Globe—it also explains the personal importance of the "magic" the speaker feels on the AP exam when she returns to E1 to find a passage from Shakespeare on the exam. Also, the writer does well in her final draft to avoid wasting her precious word count on narrating how she opened the exam booklet and looked at it. Generally, these small actions are better left implied, unless they contribute to your narrative in an important way.

Take a moment to reread the final draft of this last essay in Chapter 6. You'll also notice this tidbit of commentary gone from the final draft: "I think I should also explain that I'm eighteen years old and I still believe in magic and William Shakespeare was with me during the most magical moment of my life. I was given evidence of magic's existence when I looked down at the poetry prompt." Once again, although the student states her love of Shakespeare and her belief in magic with the kind of excitement that admission readers love to see, these statements take away from the narrative. This student's love of Shakespeare and literature is evident throughout the final draft of her essay, without these self-conscious statements. As a result, her word count stays lower, and her narrative is much more streamlined.

Quiz on Differences between
Academic Essays and Personal Essays

Take a moment to put a check mark in the Academic Essay column or in the Personal Essay column for each statement about writing. Then check your answers against the key on the following page.

	Academic Essay	**Personal Essay**
A thesis is desirable to give focus to the writing.		
Formality and structure work against desired effect of this kind of writing.		
Narrative illustrates "points" that would normally be made in the opposite kind of writing.		
Literary effect trumps having to justify your writing or to explain your meaning.		
Proof/evidence that supports claims makes your writing stronger.		

Answer Key: Quiz on Differences
between Academic Essays and Personal Essays

	Academic Essay	Personal Essay
A thesis is desirable to give focus to the writing.	x	
Formality and structure work against desired effect of this kind of writing.		x
Narrative illustrates "points" that would normally be made in the opposite kind of writing.		x
Literary effect trumps having to justify your writing or to explain your meaning.		x
Proof/evidence that supports claims makes your writing stronger.	x	

In the Moment

Once you accept that there is nothing to "prove" in a personal essay, you can allow yourself to tell your story—establish a narrative ground—either in the first line of the essay or as soon as your improved sense of narrative-lyric balance guides you to do so. Virtually all the essays in Part I seek to establish narrative in the moment early on.

With an eye toward writing in the moment, you will quickly drop your commentary and cue the actors from the start. The result is a more effective illustration of your feelings because the specific actions—the chosen moment—have to illuminate the lyric reflection and vice versa.

Write using the simple past tense or the present tense—your choice, as it is easier to establish narrative in the moment this way. Writing in the simple past or present tense will help you remain conscious of jumps between the first and second narrative moments (E1 and E2). Ineffective first attempts never establish a narrative ground. The uncertain use of tense is a major reason for this.

A Controlled Start and a Soft Landing

Concentration on writing in the moment and striking narrative-lyric balance affect and are affected by the impact of a personal essay's opening and closing lines. An engaging opening draws the reader into the moment before he or she knows it; a soft landing either makes the reader sorry that the essay has ended or surprises the reader by ending where and how it does. Particularly excellent illustrations of this technique are shown in the following essays, "The Sting of a Spelling Bee" and "Smile." The space for lyric reflection and interpretation provides a subtle soft landing and room for the reader to insert him- or herself into the narrator's personal events without gesturing overtly to their values.

At their best, even headier essays—ones that treat sexuality, family dysfunction, deaths of friends and family, or learning disabilities—find a way to understate subtly and honestly their last lines. The ability to do so indicates a writer who has recognized that, to paraphrase the famous writer Annie Dillard, the text replaces the memory.[5] That is, the text must stand coolly on its own and answer for itself to the reader—not to the memory it is supposed to represent.

Read the following essays. Although they deal with radically different content, they each put to effective use these methods of telling their stories in the moment and of starting and ending their essays in intriguing and emotional ways.

---

5. Annie Dillard, "To Fashion a Text," in *Inventing the Truth: The Art and Craft of Memoir*, ed. William Zinsser (New York: Mariner, 1998), 156.

The Sting of a Spelling Bee
Nicholas Dube

Everyone knows the feeling of standing in front of a large crowd, when it feels as if the entire world is watching and judging your every move. That fluttering that grows in the pit of your stomach and gnaws at your insides, like butterflies yearning to be set free. These butterflies are often the origin of the infamous "Uh..." that emerges from any nerve-wracked public speaker. The butterflies in my stomach grew to large bats that continually beat their wings against my insides. Suddenly it was my turn to approach the microphone, in our Scripps National Spelling Bee school-level competition.

I rose to my feet and, with a wave from the judge—our principal—stepped forward. Spelling was something that was interesting to me, and I loved to picture the words taking shape in my head, the letters lining up like soldiers to create complex troop formations such as *Cerberus* or *synthesize*. I had done well in the preceding rounds and was in the finals for my school. All that remained between me and my ticket to the regional spelling bee was one girl. She was every bit as ready to beat me, and the tension in the air was heavy. Looking out from the microphone, the bats in my stomach took flight once more and flew up into my throat. My mind was uneasy and I prepared for the worst. "Goverment," the announcer said. "Goverment. G-o-v-e-r-m-e-n-t. Goverment." I was sure of my answer. There was no way the word could be spelled any differently. Was there? A chill descended to the pit of my stomach. I glanced fervently at the judge. My heart sank as I sensed that I had somehow erred. That little bell signaled a wrong answer with a tiny *ding*, sounding the death knell of my spelling career. But wait: it was possible for me to continue on, if only the girl would misspell the same word. My spirit brightened; she looked as unsure about how to spell the word as I was. Clearly, I had spelled the word exactly how she would have. Taking my seat, I gripped the sides of the chair with an intense feeling of anxiety. My hopes were soon dashed. The announcer, who happened to be good friends with the girl's mother, said the word *government* with the slowness that would have done a sloth proud. "Gover**N**ment," she said. I was in shock; could the word be said any more obviously? The girl looked confused and asked for the word once again, and I hoped against hope that perhaps she would not understand the blatant giveaway to the word's spelling. It was not to be. Confidently, she spelled the letters of the simple word that would stick in my mind forever, a reminder of missed opportunity. "Government. G-o-v-e-r-n-m-e-n-t. Government."

(Word count: 474)

Smile[6]
Sarah R.

"Get out of my sight before I decide I'm not finished with you, bitch!" he yells as I clamber down the stairwell. I hurry down the hallway and curl up into my usual alcove, fumbling in my bag for a tool to wash the memories from my mind.

I tremble, letting the needle come to a shaky halt above my awaiting arm. It's cold, the heat in the theater's basement long having been turned off for the night. Shivering, I contemplate going back upstairs, all the while knowing it's not an option. Anything is better than running to him.

My legs—my entire body, actually—throb in agony and it's a genuine miracle I made it down the stairs in one battered but not broken piece. Fortunately there's no blood this time. Minor clothing rips can be sewn up and patched, but stains can permanently soil an otherwise perfect garment. I shake, buffeted by a wave of pain from my insides, and look warily toward the stairwell door. Will he appear again, back for more? I hope he's satisfied with the previous round of torture.

I turn my attention back to the needle and jam it into my shaking arm, letting the only refuge I've been able to find permeate my body. Salvation flows into my veins and I convulse sharply. Whoosh, and the pain begins to

---

6. Although the author of "Smile" ultimately decided not to use this essay for her college applications, it has been included here as an excellent example of the creative potential and self-understanding that can come from personal writing.

leave. I no longer think so much about the brutal encounter. Instead, the drug, the only friend offering to turn a black night into a gorgeous sunrise, carries me off.

Emerging from my cubby, my fallout shelter in the storm, I walk outside along the path to my dorm, allowing the cool winter air to serve as balm for my many wounds. I am buffeted by the wind and let it take me, control me, remove me for a few seconds from a bleak world.

When I enter my room, my roommate, a Southern girl named Ali who's a year ahead of me, is sitting at her desk. She looks up as I enter and grins.

"Your hair looks so amazing today," she comments. "I can't believe how you muster the initiative to make yourself look so beautiful. I can barely make it to class on time."

I blush. "It's nothing much," I reply.

"You're letting me take a picture of you," she orders. Nodding, I go along, too defeated by the night's events to even assert how unphotogenic I am. I look at the metal device, still in a haze from all that has happened in the past hour. I smile and urge some life into my weary eyes, because in the end, after being turned into a mere possession, it's the sole action that keeps me human. More than just some done-up mannequin in the window. More than any plastic fuck doll he could buy online.

(Word count: 476)

After you have read the previous two essays, take some time to fill
out the following chart.

	"The Sting of a Spelling Bee"	"Smile"
Tense used in essay		
Controlled start: What is it in this essay and how does it pull you in?		
Order and proportion of narrative and lyric modes (E1, E2, and L).		
Where do narrative and lyric modes begin and end in this essay?		
What is the content of the essay? What impression of the applicant does it leave you with?		
Soft landing: How does this essay end (quote directly)? How does it affect your interpretation of the essay?		
What commentary might this softer ending replace?		

In these essays, we see use of the soft landing as a form of lyric reflection. Even though the essays in this chapter are largely narrative, they each land in a subtle way that colors the reader's interpretation of them. Here again are the finishing lines for each of the two essays:

It was not to be. Confidently, she spelled the letters of the simple word that would stick in my mind forever, a reminder of missed opportunity. "Government. G-o-v-e-r-n-m-e-n-t. Government."

I smile and urge some life into my weary eyes, because in the end, after being turned into a mere possession, it's the sole action that keeps me human. More than just some done-up mannequin in the window. More than any plastic fuck doll he could buy online.

If I had to draw an overarching connection between these two essays, I'd say that they each characterize the applicants' respective situations as hopeless—that in "Smile" as particularly dire and personal but one whose resolution is suggested in those final lines. They read like the beginning of a recovery that the writer must have begun by the time she sat to write this essay. The events of "The Sting of a Spelling Bee" are more lighthearted and less consequential than those of "Smile"; all the same, their respective endings leave an opening for the reader to judge what the writers did not realize all along: they are fighting lost causes, but they also come to terms with them in controlled, wry, and understated ways.

MAXIMIZING CREATIVITY IN THE PERSONAL ESSAY

NOW THAT YOU HAVE an understanding of the key differences between academic essays and personal essays, read the essays and tips in this chapter for more on the creative possibilities of personal narrative.

Fact vs. Truth and Imaginative Language

In an essay of about five or six hundred words, you simply do not have the space to recount every detail that you would like to in your narrative or lyric reflection, so let this necessary incompleteness free you from the burden of telling things "exactly" how they happened—this factual side of things means having *too much* information to work through. The essays in Chapter 3 illustrate this tension nicely.

Even in a short essay, the urge to share "everything" can keep you from writing anything. In her essay "The Sea of Information," Andrea Barrett advises, "Facts can help *evoke* emotion, especially those that transmit texture, tonality, and sensual detail. But facts can't drive a piece." She continues: "A useful reminder [is] that the imagination is founded in, flourishes on, *images*: pictures fortified by sight, touch, taste, sounds, and passionate emotion"—imaginative language.[7]

Don't let your concern with factual and narrative completeness let

---

7. Andrea Barrett, "The Sea of Information," in *The Best American Essays 2005*, eds. Susan Orlean and Robert Atwan, The Best American Series (New York: Houghton Mifflin, 2005), 20.

commentary get in the way of reflecting, telling the narrative in the moment, and getting right to engaging starts and providing soft landings. The idea of truth in personal essay writing spans beyond factual completeness. (This is not to advocate misrepresenting yourself in your college essays. See "The Litmus Test," later in this chapter.) Rather, a writer can attempt to get at some sort of personal, emotional truth when there is *too little* information to write from. In her major essay "No Name Woman," Maxine Hong Kingston imagines competing narratives about her aunt who committed suicide back in China. As a first-generation Chinese American, Kingston explores female sexuality and seduction, her family's shame, and the suppressed narrative of the aunt, all through her bicultural identity. The facts are limited because Kingston relies on her mother's censored, shame-driven account of the aunt. But Kingston's careful emotional excavation yields her some kernel of personal truth to live by.[8]

Similarly, in the next essay, "Soar," the writer attempts to reimagine events at school while absent with a prolonged illness. (Remember Annie Dillard: The personal essay comes to replace the memory.) On the other hand, in "Deserted," the essay that follows "Soar," the writer brings to life her physical surroundings and subjective emotions by using the sort of imaginative language that Andrea Barrett prescribes. In "Man of Mystery," simple language and childlike perception work together to draw the reader into a teen's reflection on his family's past. As you read these three essays, ask yourself how the writers use imaginative language to convey their feelings about their respective situations. In the end, does it really matter whether or not their impressions are factually correct or complete? The chart at the end of the chapter provides a brief comparison of the essays for your reference. See "The Litmus Test" for more on creative license.

---

8. Maxine Hong Kingston, "No Name Woman," in *The Best American Essays of the Century*, eds. Joyce Carol Oates and Robert Atwan, The Best American Series (New York: Houghton Mifflin, 2000), 383–94.

Soar
Tom Lehmann

I could feel the silver blade slice through the vein at my elbow, and the warm red blood felt like a snail creeping down my white arm. The electric numbing agent made it tickle. They revealed the yellow spaghetti-like tube from its sterile bag and placed the end at the newly created crevice. Slowly, inch by inch, the spaghetti slithered up my vein, creating pressure deep in my shaking limb. It wiggled and heaved its way further up my arm until it hit the ninety-degree turn of my shoulder. Feeling like a small insect burrowing itself in my marrow, it made the turn and crept its way onward. They continued to push it farther, shoving it through the arteries in my chest. It burned, but I knew it was for the good. A stab at my heart, and then nothing. "It's in," the nurse said. She smiled. "Did it hurt?"

Three sicknesses in one, the doctors said. Pleural effusion, an extreme fever, and something I cannot pronounce. I remember the skin on my hands and feet all died and fell off like papier-mâché. I remember the cold, harsh metal of the walker that I used on my daily stroll. I remember the hallucinations from the penicillin; all the strange images flashing before me, in reality and dreams. A pale, clammy feel of the hospital hovered in the air, like being in a room with a heap of soap decomposing in the corner.

My sixth-grade class sent an album of their hearts. There was a picture of them holding balloons with messages to me inside of them, and they all let the balloons fly into the gusty wind. There were pictures of the school play, with another student taking over my main role. It contained a picture of my class going to the sixth-grade camping trip, climbing the rock wall with a blue sky hulking overhead. There were pictures of them smiling and giggling with excitement in the last weeks of elementary school. I could not help crying at the sight of those missed memories.

A few weeks later, I was sitting outside, gazing across the gorgeous mountain range that hugs my small hometown. There was a bee buzzing across the field I was sitting in. Then there was the humming of the black case I was required to carry with me at all times. It pumped a timed injection of penicillin through the yellow spaghetti tube into my arm, making it vibrate. I dreamed of what my fellow twelve classmates were doing as I was sitting in this field, staring at the mountains. Maybe they were in art class, creating a collage of colorful insects and animals. They could be working on the final class of 2003 mural, depicting a plane flying off into the distance, holding a banner that blared "Soar!"

(Word count: 473)

The author of "Soar" maximizes his creative license to shape a poetic strangeness from the facts of his own experience. On the one hand, he roots the reader firmly in a jarring narrative right from the start. But this factual account of medical procedure is laced with the strangeness of having to describe equipment, illness, and actions that a young boy does not understand. This lack of understanding leaves the narrator free to harness the strangeness of his experience with tight, visceral language that makes the reader squirm at the uncertainty of the boy's ordeal.

In the second paragraph, the narrator continues to make sense of his hospital surroundings, and the newness of the experience again brings to him fresh, imaginative language: "A pale, clammy feel of the hospital hovered in the air, like being in a room with a heap of soap decomposing in the corner." Along with the feeling of the spaghetti tube snaking its way into the boy's arm, the spot-on description of the stale hospital environment not only puts the reader into the scene, but also brings about pathos for the narrator's unfortunate experience as a young boy.

This intersection of the reader's sensorial and emotional involvement is at the heart of imaginative language and, therefore, at the heart of the genre of the personal essay itself. Because the young boy is essentially being acted upon, out of his element, the hallucinations from his medications open up the second half of the essay to his own poetic imaginations of what his classmates must be doing amid their normal routines, in his absence.

The transition from the medically factual ground of the first part of the essay, to the hallucinatory second part begins with this strange phrase: "My sixth-grade class sent an album of their hearts." We can assume, straightforwardly, that the narrator means that his class sent him photographs or cards with their good wishes, but there is something about the phrasing of that statement that cuts below the surface of common language.

In the last paragraph of the essay, the narrator uses these photographs as a springboard to imagine his classmates' other activities. Still, he does not let the strangeness of his reality escape us: "Then there was the humming of the black case I was required to carry with me at all times. It pumped a timed injection of penicillin through the yellow spaghetti tube into my arm, making it vibrate." The boy's clinical, limited existence is contrasted with the lovely and strange potential that he imagines for his classmates at that same moment: "They could be working on the final class of 2003 mural, depicting a plane flying off into the distance, holding a banner that blared 'Soar!'"

It's a celebratory and wishful thought that lets the narrator-as-boy forget the gloomy times he has described. Ultimately, though, whether or not his classmates are engaged in any of these activities is beside the point. The boy, for one, is hallucinating (beautifully, at that); his acts of imagination as a coping mechanism ultimately hold the truth and value for this essay.

Deserted
Eliza Gettel

I will never forget the day my mother left my brother and me to the buffalo. We were on vacation in Yellowstone, idly wandering along boardwalks, through areas rife with iridescent geothermic pools. The buffalo were also idly wandering the area, but they were not confined to the raised boardwalks like we were. Instead, they lazily ambled among the pools. We had previously been informed that wandering buffalo sometimes fell into these pools, filling the surrounding area with the unappetizing smell of steamed buffalo flesh. Even without the stench of buffalo meat, the pools reeked. They exuded a nasty, sulfurous odor that permeated the park for acres. However, the colors made the rank smell endurable. It was as if a rainbow had shattered into a million pieces and dispersed across a desolate area. There were vibrant oranges, reds, blues, and greens. The pools seemed to extend all the way into the middle of the earth. I yearned to reach out and touch the glistening surface; for fear of losing a hand, I refrained.

As we gazed into these pools, we noticed three buffalo had gathered on the hill above us. There was a male buffalo, horns and all, and a mother buffalo with a little baby buffalo. From afar, these buffalo appeared serene. They presented a stark contrast to those in a safety video we had watched in the ranger station, which had depicted unwise tourists being chased around and thrown into trees by maddened beasts. Cautious of angering them, we quickly retreated farther up the boardwalk. The buffalo now separated us from my father, who had not retreated and instead bravely (or imprudently) crossed below the herd of buffalo. He had left my brother and me with our mother farther up the boardwalk. Periodically, the buffalo would turn to stare at us with glass eyes, peering out at us from under their shaggy tresses. We finally worked up the courage to cross beneath them and rejoin my father.

We began inching our way stealthily along the boardwalk. My brother and I filed after our mother. Suddenly, the male buffalo raised his shaggy head and began charging toward us. My mother fled first. She passed around us, flailing up the boardwalk, her fanny pack flapping against her back. Her flip-flops loudly smacking against the boardwalk announced her flight clearly.

Granted, she didn't know how she would act in the situation until she was in it. She had always said she would die for us. I guess death by charging buffalo was the exception. She later claimed that she ran because she knew we could run fast and could take care of ourselves. Maybe she ran because she knew we could run faster than her. I had never seen my mother truly afraid before. It was disconcerting at first. In a strange way, though, her desertion was comforting. Her fear made her human. Before, I felt obligated to act heroically in high-pressure situations. My mother's flight showed me it's okay to lapse momentarily, that you don't always have to be strong and imperturbable. In this way, her flight also dispelled my fear of maternal duty. I had always been intimidated by people's claims that they would die for others. Needless to say, becoming a saint has never been high on my to-do list.

(Word count: 553)

Ultimately, "Deserted" is about an impromptu lesson in parental fallibility. Yet the scenic descriptions and senses are portrayed with rich and loving detail. In fact, the first third of the essay is so filled with sensory detail that the lesson reflected on in the last paragraph becomes a sort of bonus to the lovely descriptions of the scenery and wry narrative.

The first paragraph alone offers lovely descriptions. By the end of it, the writer has masterfully painted a scene. She provides visual as well as olfactory descriptions to bring the reader into that place, beautiful and smelly at once. Yellowstone comes alive, a stage on which the comic events that follow take place: "My mother fled first. She passed around us, flailing up the boardwalk, her fanny pack flapping against her back. Her flip–flops loudly smacking against the boardwalk announced her flight clearly."

This clever visual impression of the writer's mother running for her life is rounded out by the hilarious "smacking" of her flip–flops on the board-walk. The strong verb *announce* alludes to the betrayal of maternal duty. In fact, between the event of the mother's departure and the lyric reflection that follows, the writer puts to use imaginative language that does more to help the reader feel what she feels than any amount of commentary could: a mixed sense of amusement, relief, and irony. Ultimately, the language in "Deserted" touches effectively on multiple senses and emotions.

Man of Mystery
Adam Rice

When I was in middle school, my favorite uncle committed suicide. I was too young to understand why at the time, but now that I'm older, I realize that no one in the family knows. After he died, I would look into the only picture I had of him because I thought something in his face was off. I have stared into his eyes numerous times, but I have never been able to put my finger on it. My mom saw me looking at the picture one time and immediately realized who I was looking at. I was embarrassed at first, but she sat down next to me and asked, "Doesn't it look like something is off in his face?" It put me at ease to realize that I wasn't the only one who noticed something.

While looking at his face, I always remember the memories I have of him. I only have two, but I still feel that we were extremely close. The first memory is of the last Christmas we shared. I got a big present from him, and I was excited to open it because he always got me things my parents would never allow in the house. I considered him the cool uncle because of this. The present was a giant Nerf gun. I thought it was so cool because the warning said you had to be twelve to use it, and I was only ten. Another time, I was sleeping on the floor in his house, and he accidentally stepped on me because there were no lights on. I woke up, and he apologized over and over again and stayed with me until I fell back asleep.

The last thing the picture reminds me of is when my dad, my mom, and I went up to his house in Vermont the day after he died. It was snowing outside and it was mid-winter, so a decent amount of snow had already accumulated on the ground. Everyone in the family was there, supporting each other through the hard time. I was too young to comprehend everything that was happening. All I realized was that I would never get to see him again, which made me very sad. I went outside by myself and walked around in the snow. I spelled his name in the snow with my footprints. I thought it might make him magically come back. I kept on hoping for someone at the gathering to just shout, "He's alive!" Obviously, that never happened. His death is still a mystery to everyone in my family. It hurts me when I hear my younger cousins talking about how their dad died in a car accident.

(Word count: 452)

In "Man of Mystery," the imaginative language stems largely from the author's writing style itself. He reflects on his uncle's tragic end a few years afterward. The author is in high school when he sets out to write the essay, but he is still trying to come to terms with his lack of understanding of the event as he experienced it when very young.

This childlike approach emanates from simple diction and syntax: the sentences are particularly short and straightforward. He enumerates the few memories he has of his uncle, the last of which is the stunning revelation of his cousins' inability to cope with the circumstances of their loss: "His death is still a mystery to everyone in my family. It hurts me when I hear my younger cousins talking about how their dad died in a car accident."

Although the language is simple, it calls out the emotional difficulty of the crisis in precisely the way that imaginative language should. So too does the simple description in the last paragraph of the young writer trying to cope:

All I realized was that I would never get to see him ever again, which made me very sad. I went outside by myself and walked around in the snow. I spelled his name in the snow with my footprints. I thought it might make him magically come back. I kept on hoping for someone at the gathering to just shout, "He's alive!"

Such powerfully naïve descriptions of a student's world view as a child make for some of the most gripping bits of writing in literature. It is precisely this kind of impactful moment that will draw your reader closer to you as an applicant.

In the space provided, use the chart to help track the imaginative language in these three essays and its effect on you. If you'd like, you can compare your responses to the commentary that follows each essay.

	"Soar"	"Deserted"	"Man of Mystery"
Situation depicted in the essay.			
Author's attitude toward the subject.			
My response to the essay and to the author's situation.			
Imaginative language that makes me feel this way.			

Reduction

Two other useful concepts relate to establishing a sense of truth in the personal essay. The first of the two comes from Jill Ker Conway: "As a young person, it's important to scrutinize the plot you've internalized and find out whether it accurately represents what you want to be, because we tend to act out those life plots unless we think about them." The process of writing honestly, she adds, "can take parents or other figures who seem larger than life and reduce them to people in your story."⁹ Using reduction in your college essays can help you write with more narrative control.

The famous American writer James Baldwin writes in "Notes of a Native Son" about dealing with his father's death amid the Harlem race riots, his nineteenth birthday, and the birth of his

---

9. Jill Ker Conway, "Points of Departure," in *Inventing the Truth: The Art and Craft of Memoir*, ed. William Zinsser (New York: Mariner, 1998), 56.

sister.[10] Talk about larger than life: Baldwin writes that God is marking his father's death with major, unrelated events. Such is the power of Baldwin's father over him. Yet through honest and masterful writing, Baldwin manages to reduce the omnipotent patriarch to a few essential traits, to manage him on paper, while the essence of the piece drifts amorphously. The focus on his father's bitterness in particular helps Baldwin confront his own.

In the earlier essay, "Deserted," the writer, in addition to providing rich, imaginative descriptions of her Yellowstone adventure, successfully manages to reduce her mother to a "size" fitting for reflection on paper, changing the writer's own perceptions of what it means to be a good parent. The same can be said of any number of the essays in Part I—"Off the Table," "December 24th," "Fenway," and "Rosalie's Move," for example.

Style before Content

In addition to reduction, *style before content* holds that effectively saying what you can is more important than saying everything you want to. In a very technical way, style before content guides all the discussed points, although it also helps you write a smooth and effective personal narrative. It means deciding what the essay is and isn't "about," choosing relevant narrative moments, and effectively reducing real-life figures to manageable, identifiable traits. Locally, it means writing concise sentences that cut down on weak structural forms like excessive prepositional phrases and dangling modifiers. From sentence to sentence, paragraph to paragraph, and page to page, style before content serves to focus the main relationship at hand and what you, the writer, want to say about it. The marked-up essay drafts in Chapter 7 speak to the difficulties of letting content go in the name of a more streamlined essay.

In the following essays, these writers each reduce figures in their respective essays to manageable characters on the page without

---

10. James Baldwin, "Notes of a Native Son," in *The Best American Essays of the Century*, 220–38.

oversimplifying their situations. They also choose—among all the statements that they could make and details that they could provide—the most effective to make their stories move.

Take a look at the following essay, "The Darkness." How does the author effectively reduce his parents to manageable characters in his story? What are the traits that he reduces them to? What is the effect of this reduction, and how does it help him tell a cohesive story?

The Darkness
C. H. Martin

One night upon returning from work, he welcomed us with lavish gifts. This seemed strange to the both of us, but we graciously accepted the tokens of love. I didn't recognize at the time that the look on my mother's face was that of concern for my father. They went into the other side of the house and sat down in front of the television to watch the news. My brother and I, in the meantime, ran up to our rooms to play with the new gifts.

Later that evening when I had grown bored of the video game, I went down to sit with my mom and dad in the living room. My brother, on the other hand, remained in his room. Upon entering the living room, I saw only my mother sitting there in the rocking recliner, watching the evening news. She had asked me what I was doing down there instead of up playing with my new game. My response was simple: that I wanted to spend time with them watching TV.

She just shook her head and continued to watch the weather. As I sat across from her on the couch, I began to wonder where my dad had gone. I took a quick glimpse into the kitchen when my mom wasn't looking, but I couldn't find him. So I told my mom that I was going to go off and get a drink from the fridge, and she told me to bring a drink for her as well. On the way to the basement (that is where the fridge with the drinks was), I saw my dad off in the computer room, just looking at the weather and sport scores.

In the basement, I thought that my dad might be thirsty and also want a drink so I grabbed an extra drink from the fridge for my dad. On the way up from the basement, I heard a weird sound come from the direction of the computer room. So on my way in to give my dad the drink, I realized that he was playing a game on the computer with the lights turned down low. I held out the drink and asked if he wanted it. He took the drink with a slight thanks and nothing more. Then I had asked what he was doing and he merely said, "Playing a game."

I left the room feeling slightly puzzled and brought my mom her drink. I then returned to my seat on the couch. A minute or two later, I looked at my mom and asked why Dad sat alone in the computer room so much and she just shook off the question as if it were never asked. I repeated the question, only a little louder as not to alert my dad, and the answer was the same. None.

At that point, I realized that that was just how he was and I went back to my room, alone, to play with my video games in the dark.

(Word count: 507)

"The Darkness" begins ominously with this title and extends into a simple, well-framed narrative that effectively characterizes the narrator's home life in a very short space.

From the start of the narrative, the parents, presented through the young narrator's nonjudgmental observations, "reveal themselves." In choosing the story that he will tell, the narrator lets the important traits of his parents and home life surface on their own. (We might each think of how we'd be perceived by a stranger, depending on the situation in which we are being observed. In two selected moments, observers might take us each for two entirely different people.)

In the narrative selected by the author to share, the parents are at odds in a fundamental way that affects the basic function of the family: "One night upon returning from work, he welcomed us with lavish gifts. This seemed strange to the both of us, but we graciously accepted the tokens of love. I didn't recognize at the time that the look on my mother's face was that of concern for my father."

Is the mother angry at the father for spending money that the family doesn't have? Does she think the father is trying to buy their sons' love? Is she jealous of the close relationship that the father has with the boys? Or has the father done something terrible that he is now trying to make up for the best he knows how?

There is just no telling, but what ensues in the narrative takes precedence over the cause of the parents' spat: the children "are left in the dark"—uncertain and rejected by their parents, who are unable to communicate with each other about their problems. Ultimately, they take these frustrations out on their sons and isolate themselves at opposite ends of the house.

Despite the desperation of the family's situation, the narrator maturely limits himself to merely reporting on the situation from a child's perspective: "I left the room feeling slightly puzzled and brought my mom her drink," he writes, without judgment. A little further in the essay: "A minute or two later, I looked at my mom and asked why Dad sat alone in the computer room so much and she just shook off the question as if it were never asked. I repeated the question, only a little louder as not to alert my dad, and the answer was the same. None."

Although the narrator never pities himself or condemns his parents' behavior in this essay, the reader must feel deeply for this young man who tries to make sense of an adult situation that even the adults cannot confront. He could find himself in the hopeless role of peacemaker or of model child; just as sad, he resigns himself to the feckless family network into which he has been born.

The image that he ends with—four family members, each in a different room of the dark house, each before an illuminated screen—is saddening because it says more about the family's circumstances than anything he could write about it directly. A movie camera, perhaps on a crane, seems to pan away from this house as a vision of the loneliness that must reside there.

Good-Byes
Anonymous

The girl was staring more intently at the glowing television than any person I had ever seen, yet she could hardly comprehend the intricacies of *Grey's Anatomy*. I watched the gears grinding in her head as she tried hopelessly to understand the characters of the popular television show. At last, I decided to retire to sleep, chuckling to myself in the knowledge that she would be up for hours trying to analyze the plot of the show.

"Good night, Sofia," I said.

"Bye," was her simple response.

Sofia had come from Torreblanca, Spain, a petite, hunched-over exchange student; the traditional Spanish braid of her hometown hung at her hip. Her braid was a damp vine tangled with scents from the jungle. My mother and I begged her to cut it, but we were met by indignant refusal. I took to pretending that Sofia did not exist, and I continued my life as I had before she arrived.

At the end of the first night Sofia arrived in the United States from Spain, I said "good night" to her. She did not respond. Initially I was not bothered by her rudeness. I assumed that she did not hear me or that she did not understand my English. After a week of no responses, I grew frustrated. I asked her why she never responded when I said "good night." She told me that in Spain, saying "good night" to someone meant that you would not see them again. She noticed my frustration, however, and decided that she would respond to my "good nights" with the word *bye*.

One weekend, my parents went on vacation and Sofia and I were left alone in the house. On Friday night, Sofia and I had a fight and she ran crying to her room. By Sunday night, I realized that I had not seen Sofia for the entire weekend. I began to grow concerned and went to check on her.

Sofia's hand was broken and bleeding. She had punched the wall in her rage against me. Her face was clenched with pain, the muscles of her cheeks tight, preventing tears from rolling down her face. I did not speak to her during the ride to the hospital. Her cast was a barrier, and I was happy to have it there.

I took Sofia to have the cast removed. Her English had improved since the incident, and she and I were able to have limited conversations on the way to the hospital. At Christmas, Sofia suddenly cut the braid from her hair. At first it was hard to recognize her, but gradually I forgot about the foul-smelling tangle that had defined her for so many months. We established mutually beneficial agreements: I would do her English homework if she would do my Spanish homework. At long last, I considered her a friend.

Sofia cried as she boarded her plane home to Spain.

"Good-bye," she said.

"Bye, Sofia," I responded. I really meant it.

(Word count: 497)

As is the case with any narrative, this author must select just a couple of representative snippets of his months with a foreign-exchange student to give a picture in this essay of their time together. The author's reduction of the Spanish student is carefully constructed around the moments that he chooses to depict and the characteristics that he uses to describe the Spanish student: her long braid, poor English, jungle scent, and, of course, "bye."

Once these traits are established, they quickly characterize the relationship between Sofia and the narrator in the essay—their strangeness to each other, their language barrier, and the narrator's condescension. All these dynamics are in place by the end of the second long paragraph, at which point the narrator writes her off: "I took to pretending that Sofia did not exist, and I continued my life as I had before she arrived."

This early conclusion marks the end of the exposition of the essay and leads next to the climax of the narration, when the young girl breaks her hand while home alone with the narrator, and they must deal with the ordeal on their own.

On an optimistic beat, the narrator decides to conclude the essay with a series of adaptations that his guest has made by the end of her trip. Without coming off as ethnocentric, he mentions how much her English has improved and pays her the compliment of noting a better hairdo. In fact, they become partners in crime, helping each other with homework in their native languages. "At long last," the narrator shares, "I considered her a friend."

Even had he not explicitly shared this change in their relationship, he hints at a change in their rapport by carefully choosing to bid her farewell in her customary manner, an effective symbolic action to end with.

The following chart compares how the two previous authors reduce their subjects to characters on the page, to give you a sense of how to reduce people effectively in your essays.

	"The Darkness"	**"Good–Byes"**
People reduced	Parents	Spanish student Sofia
Reductive traits	Silence, separate rooms, TV/computer, strange looks	Broken English, long braid, jungle scent, fit of anger
Style before content in narrative	One evening described in household	Watching TV, saying good night, vacation/ ER visit, departure

The Litmus Test

Fact vs. truth as a tool is extremely useful for opening up the possibilities of the genre of the personal essay to make the most of the short space typically available for college application essays. The idea of being completely and factually accurate has several drawbacks and is, in fact, not practical when you have so much riding on such a short piece of personal narrative.

For one, making statement after statement about a personal experience can be far more bland, redundant, and monotonous than grounding an essay about this personal experience in a controlled narrative. Second, a narrative, including a proportional amount of lyric reflection, has the paradoxical effect of making it easier to fill a word-limit essay and to fit in the key information you want to share about yourself, while making the reading experience pass more smoothly for your admissions audience. In a beneficial way—to the writer and to the reader—the narrative-based personal essay becomes both longer and shorter at once.

Annie Dillard's notion of fashioning a text, while giving the writer a great deal of freedom, also gives the author a great deal of responsibility.[11] Where there are endlessly debated ethical issues at play in a responsibly told personal narrative, there is the added one of academic honesty in presenting yourself in a truthful light to a college or university.

Knowingly misrepresenting the contents of your life in an application essay clearly falls under the umbrella of unethical writing and academic dishonesty. For example, claiming as your own an experience that is not yours falls under this umbrella. However, using all the poetic and creative devices available to the personal essayist allows the writer to shrug off the tedium of "reporting" every detail of an experience or memory. As long as you are aware of and honest with yourself about this difference, you can maximize the creative possibilities of personal narrative. Your experiences become the basis for the creative exploration and sharing of a narrative moment.

This is also where literary effect—conveying to readers how an experience *feels* through the way you write about it—is at its most useful. The personal essay fills this gap by giving someone who would otherwise remain a statistic in a news story the opportunity to convey in a deep and heartfelt manner the emotions of the experience behind newsprint.

What this means for you as a college applicant is the opportunity to emerge from the statistics—from the flood of paper applications at thousands of colleges and universities across the country, and from the bland factualness of reporting personal events impersonally and journalistically—to stand out amid other applicants and to convey the full importance of your personal experiences to your readers in the fundamental way that only narrative affords. In short, the litmus test for the truthfulness of the personal essay is whether you recognize your life in it.

---

11. Dillard, "To Fashion a Text," 156.

OTHER COMPOSITIONAL CONSIDERATIONS

A Note on Risk

In this day and age, most adults recognize the increasing complexities that adolescents face. They understand that this is not the world in which they grew up, and they don't expect to read about fond, carefree memories from essay to essay. That said, applicants should not feel compelled to sugarcoat or omit their defining experiences in their application essays, even when these experiences are sensitive, unusual, odd, or painful. In fact, as mentioned before, content of this sort can lend itself to a richly expressive personal essay. Some essays included in this manual—"Smile," "Man of Mystery," "Some Fancy Name," "The Darkness"—treat sensitive personal matters. Their authors do so successfully by structuring sensitive material the same as they would more lighthearted stuff. Abstractly, if you were to erase from these essays their content, you would find underneath the same important qualities that other sample essays here demonstrate: narrative-lyric balance, narrative told in the moment, widening lyric reflection, reduction, imaginative language, and style emphasized before content. In theory, these essays would each be used to treat a relevant application prompt.

There is advice to the contrary, that you should show no sign of weakness in your college essay. Some parents have expressed similar concerns to me about their students' essays. I can't help but ask, if a university wants to know about you as an applicant, and the story that comes to your mind isn't the rosiest, would you really be sharing yourself if you did not write about it? The genre of the personal essay—narrative—offers sophisticated ways of handling "negative" material. No matter the content, you can still show yourself to be a great writer and complex personality.

A well-written, conscientious essay will deliver no matter the content, and the well-earned four-letter word can, in fact, add to your narrative and earn you points for successful risk taking. On the other hand, irresponsible use of language and controversial content that does not help paint a more complex and intriguing portrait of the writer can very well cause an essay to be dismissed on those grounds. My advice to students applying to selective colleges: you might as well venture out on your own terms, but be sure to do so tactfully and responsibly. Here are a few reminders to keep in mind when sitting down to write about sensitive personal material for a college essay:

DON'T

- Exploit your own experiences for the sake of "being different" or standing out.
- Feel like you have to write about some large or intimate experience to write a meaningful or successful essay.
- Use the real names of people who are implicated in sensitive material.
- Write to shock.
- Write about something you cannot wrap a satisfactory narrative around.
- Write about something that you are not comfortable sharing with strangers.
- Write about something that does not paint you in a thoughtful or complex light.
- Fear being judged, remembered, or identified by an honest essay, should you attend the college for which it is used.
- Resign your sensitive material to a "lessoned learned."

- Embellish or misrepresent the facts of your own circumstances.[12]

DO

- Keep in mind the social conservativeness of the school when choosing to write about sensitive personal material and how to frame it.
- Keep in mind the selectivity of the school (the more selective the school, the more risk you might consider taking in your writing, to the degree you are comfortable doing so).
- Make sure that your essay reflects your application in its entirety.[13]

Avoiding Cliché Essays

Just as you don't want your essay to stand out for the wrong reasons, you don't want it to sink in with the thousands of others either. Most university application prompts are vague precisely to elicit a wide range of responses from a large applicant pool. It becomes the task of the college hopeful to liven up the response pool for overworked admissions officials. By sticking to narrative and employing any combination and proportion of the suggestions in this manual, you place yourself in a better position to avoid writing cliché essays for your college applications. You can achieve this by:

- Responding to an application prompt with a narrative, which allows you to focus on writing a cohesive personal essay ("fashioning a text") instead of "answering a prompt."
- Avoiding the temptation to suggest how the events of your narrative will translate to your success in college (unless the prompt specifically tells you to do this).
- Letting this narrative-based personal essay address the prompt associatively without succumbing to the false need for a justifying thesis or

---

12. See "The Litmus Test" in Chapter 8.

13. For strategies on which essay to use for a specific application, see Appendix 3: Matching Essays with Applications.

self-conscious commentary to "support a main idea" or to "answer" the prompt.

- Creating a sense of control through narrative-lyric proportion and vivid imaginative language.
- Avoiding tackling impossibly large topics (e.g., death, success, family, love, faith, class, sexuality, race, disability, politics) head on and by focusing instead on a narrative that carries some hint of your thoughts on any of these larger issues in the specifics of the event(s) you frame.

In short, in terms of the structural points given in this manual, you risk submitting a cliché essay when you do not stick to the momentary specifics of a carefully chosen narrative and the subtlety of delicate reflection. *Avoiding cliché essays is not simply a matter of content but a matter of how you structure your content.* You need only search "clichés" or "cliché essays" online to get an idea for what they are—but you already know them. For good measure, a couple of varieties are *I lost but learned* and *Sports have prepared me for success on and off the field.* There are many others—the point is that clichés are worn out and predictable for the reader. The essay drafts in Chapter 7 help draw the distinction between clichés and imaginative language.

In the well-structured personal essay, virtually any topic goes. One general topic to be more careful with, though, is sports. For one, if you are an athlete on one of your high school's teams, this fact will show up elsewhere in your application materials. (If you want to compete as a college athlete, see Appendix 8: Interview with a Stanford Student-Athlete Alumnus.) You can certainly write a great sports-themed essay, but you should avoid attempting to link athletic success to academic success in college. Sports are incredibly important in American culture and touch on so many other social, cultural, and political issues. If you want to write about your athletics, you might consider how your experiences in sports touch on some of these broader issues.[14] Whatever your subject matter,

---

14. ESPN's 30 for 30 documentary film series offers excellent discussions of sports in this light. Consider viewing one or two of these films before you write a sports essay.

actively engaging with Andrea Barrett's notion of imaginative language will keep your expressions more fresh, lively, and effective.

Strategies for Word Limits

You have undoubtedly noticed that some of the essays in this book come in at longer than five hundred words. While CA4, the newest Common Application, requires a word count of between 250 and 650 words, the old version—for which many of these essays were written— had a five-hundred-word limit. Even though the word limit is higher now, you should still try trimming your narratives to as close to five hundred words as you can.

Although we cannot say what the word limit might be for any of these essays' corresponding prompts, let's assume for a moment that they all had to answer to a five-hundred-word limit.

Odds are that once you try out the strategies spelled out here, you will consistently be able to come pretty close to the official word limit without compromising the content or essence of your essay.

Generally, students who complain about not being able to get their essays going or about not coming close to the word limit of an admissions essay are not grounding their essays in narrative. If this is your case, revisit "The Litmus Test" in Chapter 8 and Chapters 6 and 7 on how to frame a narrative.

Many college applicants who have completed a rough draft of an essay struggle with cutting the length down to under the allotted word limit. Commonly, they look at their completed drafts, mystified at how they will chop off so much important information just to reach a specified word count. This can be extremely frustrating, so here are a few tips to help you deal with meeting word counts:

- While drafting, don't worry about the word count as you write. Instead, you should focus on following the guidelines for establishing one or two narrative moments in an essay and then moving on to provide lyric reflection for this narrative. Compulsive preoccupation with the word count while drafting will affect your ability to focus on writing smoothly and will take up more time.

- Instead of making content choices based on the allotted word count, compose your essay according to the cohesiveness of the narrative you are trying to establish and according to the literary effect you seek.

- Once you have finished drafting (and have taken a break from the essay), revisit your essay. Identify the first narrative event and, if applicable, the second narrative event and the lyric reflection. Mark these specifically (I recommend editing a printed draft), so that you can identify any part of your essay that does not belong to the key narrative and lyric portions of the essay. (For example, do you wander into a third narrative moment that your first two wouldn't miss if deleted?) Delete any information that does not fall into one of these three elements.

- At this point, you can check the word count in your word-processing software if you'd like to, just to get an idea of how much more deleting you might have to do. Remember that while your essay might come in at 499 words (assuming a five-hundred-word limit), there could be other deletions that would improve the focus and flow of your narrative. Keep in mind Annie Dillard: "fashion a text" (not "meet a word count").[15]

- If you are still over the word limit but content with the way the essay is constructed, you are going to have to start making some difficult editing choices. Following this chart can help you move closer to both the word limit and the best narrative you can write:

---

15. Dillard, "To Fashion a Text," 156.

	Hatchet	Scalpel
Step 1	If your word count is seventy-five words or more above the limit, then delete the least important paragraph in your essay.	If your word count is down to just twenty-five words or so above the limit, then begin deleting prepositional phrases and wordy phrasing.
Step 2	If your word count is fifty to seventy-five words or more above the limit, then delete the least important sentences in your essay, one by one.	Next, consider deleting adjectives and adverbs as needed.
Step 3	For reference: the preceding bulleted paragraph that begins with "At this point" contains seventy-five words.	After any deletions, check for awkward phrasing and transitional elements to patch things up.

Meeting Character Limits

Maybe it's the effect of new social media; some institutions now have character limits for their writing components. In addition to following the tips on the previous pages, you can consider the following when preparing an essay for which a character limit is set:

- Conduct a find-and-replace-all search for double spaces, replacing them with single spaces—yes, even after periods. This is the standard in publishing, and your admissions reader won't think twice about it, if s/he notices it at all.

- As needed, replace longer words with shorter synonyms while maintaining a natural tone.
- Delete indentations/combine paragraphs.
- Get rid of conjunctions and create separate sentences or use the occasional semicolon (but be sure to review its usage).
- If you are still far over the character limit, remove the least important sentences, one by one, until you reach the desired character count.
- Be sure to reread after any deletion or rephrasing to check for awkward expression.
- As a point of reference: the two bulleted paragraphs, on the previous pages, that begin with "Once you have finished" and "At this point," have a combined word count of 172 and a combined character count of 989 (with spaces).
- Conduct a spelling and grammar check only once you have made the above edits and then adjust as needed. (Be sure to conduct the check *slowly and carefully*.)

Choosing a Title

Many college applications—whether they subscribe solely to the Common Application, to the Common Application with supplemental materials, or use independent application forms—generally require a long essay (say, five hundred words) and shorter writing components of between two hundred and three hundred words (or a comparable character count). The principal essay in a college application should carry a title, while the shorter pieces generally need not (you can certainly add a title if you have one in mind even for a short essay).

If you have a title that you like for your essay, then trust your gut and use it. But if you are struggling to find a fitting title, you can try a few things:

- Ask readers for suggestions.
- Use a singular phrase from the essay as the title.

- List ideas over the course of a few days.
- Give the essay a title that is broad enough to suggest what it is about.

If you take a look at the titles of the essays included in this manual, a lot of them are straightforward: they serve their purpose without getting too clever and without taking away from the personal essays that follow them. In short, they are sensible: "December 24th," "The Darkness," "Balance," "Man of Mystery." Not exactly eye-popping stuff, but maybe that's the point—you want the title to provide a gentle lead into the narrative, so that the essay can do its work.

There are obviously a couple of exceptions in this manual: "The Sting of a Spelling Bee" and "On Receiving a Gift from a 445-Year-Old Dead Man." These titles are, well, clever, and more importantly, they work. The tone of the light pun in "The Sting of a Spelling Bee" is maintained throughout the piece. The reverence that the narrator feels for Shakespeare is present from the get-go in the title of "On Receiving a Gift from a 445-Year-Old Dead Man," and it continues throughout.

But just because you can make a pun doesn't mean you should. And as annoying as it can be to delay giving your essay a title, take a few days to think about it if one does not come immediately to mind. When and where you do go for a pun or whimsical title, make sure that it suits your essay as a whole.

Campus Narratives

Application prompts that ask some version of "Why our school?" are ripe for narrative-based responses that can play to a number of strengths in the genre of the personal essay. First, it is vital to note that when schools ask applicants to respond to this sort of question, they are gauging each applicant's suitability for and genuine interest in what they have to offer their students. They are not searching for compliments.[16]

---

16. See Appendix 7: Interview with an Ivy League Interviewer.

As a student of the personal essay, you are extremely well equipped to field this sort of prompt: *What interests you about X University? Describe a trait or experience that would make you a good match for our school. What do you have to contribute to our campus community?* Many applicants lose their cool in the face of questions like this. They let their eagerness—and anxiety—about admissions show in their responses: *X University would be a perfect match for me because...I would love to go to such a prestigious university.*

Institutions are looking for qualified responses to separate one applicant from the next. Instead of flattering the school admissions officials—who already know you are eager to attend, since you have put out the time, money, and hope to apply in the first place—use the application space to *make them* want you to attend their school too. Of course, this isn't to suggest that you should hide your enthusiasm at the idea of attending a school.

Here's your trump card: take the time to research the school—campus map, names of dorms and corresponding dining commons, photos, natural/urban surroundings, clubs that interest you (or that are lacking, so that you can essentially propose one), course titles, campus buildings, professors. Then write a narrative in which you place yourself convincingly—via this research—right in the school community in a way that frames your interests, speaks to your background, and makes use of what you and a particular school have to offer *each other*.

You can do this by narrating a day in your life at this school of interest—waking up and conversing with your roommate from another part of the country, walking out of such-and-such freshman dormitory to go eat at the most likely dining commons. Are you running late? Is it near or far to your first class? How are you doing in this course so far, and who is the professor? How does this class fit in with your plans for your major? Do you have a crush on anyone in the class? Is the course venue a large lecture hall or an intimate seminar room? Later, do you go on to another class? A lab? Lunch? Whom do you eat with? How's the food? Do you eat on campus or go to a local hangout? And most importantly, how have you adjusted in your time on this campus so far?

You obviously don't have to answer each and every one of these questions. Rather, choose one or two narrative moments to illustrate. The more details you can knowledgeably share about a campus and its community, the more effectively you will be able to state your case for admission to a school. The more vividly you can picture yourself on a campus, the better the chance your admissions audience will be able to picture you there too. See the essays in Chapter 5 for models.

Short Responses and Non-Narrative Responses

Supplemental writing on an application does not have to go the way of the personal essay. If you can give a brief narrative to a short prompt (say, two hundred to three hundred words), then go for it. Sometimes a short supplemental prompt will ask why you want to attend that college or university. This might be a reasonable opportunity to write a condensed narrative of a campus visit, for example.

If you feel like it would not be appropriate to respond to a supplemental prompt with a narrative, provide a straightforward, informed, and concise response. For example, a high school student with a strong background in computer coding, artistic methods, or engineering wants to bring evidence of this knowledge into focus on a prompt that asks about areas of study that are of interest at a college or university. Clearly, that doesn't mean that you need to narrate yourself typing at the keyboard. Whether you go the way of narrative here or not, implementing your research about a school's undergraduate research programs and academic facilities can help your cause. It also doesn't hurt to mention faculty you could see yourself working with or to key in on campus tradition. See the essays in Chapter 5 for models.

Optional Essays

Are they a trap? Will it be held against you if you do not respond to optional prompts? No, optional means *optional*. Optional prompts are spaces that invite you to offer anything about yourself that the application has not given you the opportunity to share are there for you to provide as complete, accurate, and favorable a portrait of yourself as you can. If you cannot think of additional, relevant information to provide in these spaces, do not rattle your brain for the sole sake of filling the space, and do not stress over what to put.

That said, for particularly competitive schools (you know which ones) with optional application prompts, it is worth your time to approach these, especially if they deal with academic topics and not simply personal ones. Highly selective schools will likely see a crowded, competitive field respond to optional questions of an academic nature.

Optional application prompts that inquire about extenuating or unusual personal circumstances are there for applicants who have achieved academic viability under uncommon conditions. If this applies to you, then you should answer these prompts in a truthful and straight-forward manner. I suggest that these questions are not essay prompts like the others. Instead, think of them as surveys and answer them journalistically—just the facts. If you do feel a narrative coming on when responding to these optional essays, see how it goes and make your decision based on the criteria listed.

Again, take your time in generating material for these types of questions, especially academic ones. Whether the optional prompts you encounter are academic or personal in nature, do not force a response if you do not feel that it provides a more complete depiction of your profile.

SOME FINAL THOUGHTS

T HE APPLICATION SEASON HAS become a grueling rite of passage for many college-bound students, and an entire industry has sprung up around this rite. Even this book, which earnestly seeks to alleviate some of that pressure, is still a marker of that industry and intensity. It may prove challenging for you as a high school student to find the time to read this book in its entirety, simply because the lives of young people seem to grow busier and more complex as the years roll on. There is so much for young people to navigate without the looming pressures of college admissions.

But I do hope that this book will recast the admissions process in a more humanistic light, starting with recognition of your role in the process. The language we use to describe the admissions gauntlet can be so disempowering: *University X rejected me*, *I got wait-listed by College Y*, and *I've been accepted to University Z*. This kind of shorthand is understandable because a physical campus community is a college applicant's desired goal and destination, and we tend to give this looming, impersonal entity so much power over the futures we see for ourselves. It's important to remember that real people care very much about which applicants they are opening up their campus communities to, and that the story you tell about yourself can have a very real impact on those people's decisions.

College admissions is also a business. Colleges and universities have a given number of seats they need to fill each year and profiles in mind of certain types of students with which to fill them. They need band members, student organizers, work-study recipients, and athletes. And these criteria change from year to year. Measuring, ranking, monetizing, and scrutinizing every aspect of admissions, colleges are intensely aware of how their public reputations and competitiveness on the admissions market affect their quotas.

Yet I've heard it said that college applicants are more selective than institutions. And there is some truth to that if you think about it. Students apply to only a few schools and select just one to attend. Colleges, on the other hand, offer admission to a large number of applicants, anticipating that an estimated percentage will accept and fill their quota of seats. And you can be sure that universities won't take your rejection personally. Admissions officers may have their favorite applicants, but they probably don't get their hopes up about individual applicants the way high school students do about dream schools. When you think about it, many students base their ideas of dream schools on simple impressions—a brand name, a reputation, a geographic location, a campus visit, a vibe. Bear in mind that any of these impressions can disappoint—or surprise—in the long run, especially as you grow and evolve throughout the application process and as an undergraduate.

The more I've thought about college admissions as a business model, the more convinced I've become of the role personal narrative can play in it. There is the fundamental lesson here that in this complex and multifaceted process, college hopefuls can control only so much. Yes, the creative points put forward in this book will help you write better personal statements for your college applications. But using personal narrative to rethink who you are and what your life has meant to this point can deepen the significance of the admissions process beyond which schools accept you. At its best, this personal process will affect what you write about in college essays and even where you decide to go to school, because personal writing can change in no small part who you are.

In short, the features of personal narrative speak to the demands of the admissions process while providing you with a manageable space in which to address the many factors that are out of your hands. If you can embrace this process and aim for personal discovery in your writing, then I believe the rest will fall more easily into place. And once you've made it through the admissions process, I hope you will continue writing to make sense of the world as you venture out with confidence.

Thank you for taking the time to read this book, and best of luck.

—JTN

APPENDIX 1

ESSAY QUESTIONS YOU MIGHT SEE

T HE APPLICATION ESSAY IS growing in importance. In fact, some schools value the essay over GPAs or standardized test scores in an effort to differentiate so many competitive applicants nowadays. To do this, colleges are asking more provocative questions in an attempt to get to know the personality behind the transcript. The Common Application's 2013 move to a single personal statement of up to 650 words clearly speaks to the increased importance of the essay too. The first group of essay prompts consists of some recent examples that admissions departments are developing to tease out an applicant's personality. When faced with unconventional prompts like these, use the techniques from this book to organize your response and add a little imagination. These unusual prompts are followed by several that are more conventional and tame. Whichever type your schools ask, the sample essays in this book and your knowledge of personal narrative will guide you well in your response.

Unusual

Sartre said, "Hell is other people," but Streisand sang, "People who need people/Are the luckiest people in the world." With whom do you agree and why? —Amherst College

———

If you could choose to be raised by robots, dinosaurs, or aliens, who would you pick? Why? —Brandeis University

———

If you were reduced to living on a flat plane, what would be your greatest problems? Opportunities? —Hamilton College

———

Using a piece of wire, a Hopkins car window sticker, an egg carton, and any inexpensive hardware store item, create something that would solve a problem. Tell us about your creation, but don't worry; we won't require proof that it works! —Johns Hopkins University

———

What invention would the world be better off without, and why? —Kalamazoo College

———

Tell us about the most embarrassing moment of your life. —Santa Clara University

———

St. Mary's College is casting for the incoming class. Send us your audition tape via the Web or DVD. Please provide us with the site for posting. Selection of this option will stand as your college essay. Consider your audience. —St. Mary's College of Maryland

———

Create a short story using one of these topics: "The End of MTV," "Confessions of a Middle School Bully," "The Professor Disappeared," or "The Mysterious Lab." —Tufts University

———

Kermit the Frog famously lamented, "It's not easy being green." Do you agree? —Tufts University

———

Have you ever walked through the aisles of a warehouse store like Costco or Sam's Club and wondered who would buy a jar of mustard a foot and a half tall? We've bought it, but it didn't stop us from wondering about other things, like absurd eating contests, impulse buys, excess, unimagined uses for mustard, storage, preservatives, notions of bigness…and dozens of other ideas both silly and serious. Write an essay somehow inspired by super-huge mustard. —University of Chicago

———

So where is Waldo, really? —University of Chicago

———

You have 150 words. Take a risk. —University of Notre Dame

———

You have just finished your three-hundred-page autobiography. Please submit page 217. —University of Pennsylvania

———

Make a bold prediction about something in the year 2020 that no one else has made a bold prediction about. —University of Virginia

Conventional

Some students have a background or story that is so central to their identity that they believe their application would be incomplete without it. If this sounds like you, then please share your story.

Recount an incident or time when you experienced failure. How did it affect you, and what lessons did you learn?

Reflect on a time when you challenged a belief or idea. What prompted you to act? Would you make the same decision again?

Describe a place or environment where you are perfectly content. What do you do or experience there, and why is it meaningful to you?

Discuss an accomplishment or event, formal or informal, that marked your transition from childhood to adulthood within your culture, community, or family. —Common Application (CA4)

———

Describe the world you come from—for example, your family, community, or school—and tell us how your world has shaped your dreams and aspirations. —UC Berkeley

———

Undergraduates at Emory and Oxford Colleges are offered countless opportunities to engage with the student body, the faculty, and your academic program of choice—from hands-on research to student organizations to volunteering. What are some of the programs and/or activities you would plan to get involved with on either campus, and what unique qualities will you bring to them? —Emory University

———

What are the unique qualities of Northwestern—and of the specific undergraduate school to which you are applying—that make you want to attend the University? In what ways do you hope to take advantage of the qualities you have identified? —Northwestern University

———

A range of academic interests, personal perspectives, and life experiences adds much to the educational mix. Given your personal background, describe an experience that illustrates what you would bring to the diversity in a college community or an encounter that demonstrated the importance of diversity to you. —Stevens Institute

———

The strength of the University of Maryland is realized through the contributions of every member of our campus. We understand each individual is a result of his/her personal background and experiences. Describe the parts that add up to the sum of you. —University of Maryland

———

Please briefly elaborate on one of your extracurricular activities or work experiences. —Vanderbilt University

APPENDIX 2

STRATEGIES FOR BRAINSTORMING PERSONAL MATERIAL

WHEREAS WRITING BIOGRAPHY DEALS with the problem of too little information, writing autobiographical material deals with the problem of too much information: *I am a complex person, too complex to be reduced to transcripts, letters of recommendation, and word limits in a college application.* In other words, you become aware of your own limitations in the high-stakes circumstances of college admissions. Then again, so does everyone.

Before you even get to the stage of framing your well-chosen narrative events on paper, you will need some time to decide what to write about—naturally. If you are not overflowing with ideas for narratives that capture you in your unique light, then you might consider one or more of the following suggestions to get the narrative going:

- Keep a journal or even a simple list of potential essay narratives.
- Don't let your critical side (the editor within) start criticizing your writing before you even get started—give yourself permission to write freely.
- Read through old personal diaries or journals to remember important events and the way they felt to you at the time.
- Visit old hangouts to relive the feelings and memories associated with prior experiences.

- Browse photo albums to jog your memory.
- Ask close friends and relatives to recount their defining memories of you (let them be honest).
- Read in the genre of the personal essay.[17]

These suggestions stem from the notion that often we take our own circumstances and idiosyncrasies for granted because, well, they are ours and always have been. Aspects of our lives as individuals could be of great interest to readers—if only we made ourselves aware of them first. For the same reason you want to ground your essays in narrative—to connect with your (admissions) readers in the most fundamental of human ways—engaging in the warm-up activities will bring to mind stories. The right story has a way of making itself known—maybe not right away and maybe not in the first draft. But narrative is contagious: stories give way to stories, and objects help us recollect, even when we aren't necessarily looking to remember anything. This is how memory works.

---

17. See Appendix 9: *Easy Being Green* Online for more on suggestions.

APPENDIX 3

MATCHING ESSAYS WITH APPLICATIONS

Here are partial instructions for the new Common Application personal statement (expanded in 2013 from a range of 250 to 500 words to a range of 250 to 650 words): "The essay demonstrates your ability to write clearly and concisely on a selected topic and help you distinguish yourself in your own voice. *What do you want the readers of your application to know about you apart from courses, grades, test scores?*...Remember: 650 words is your limit, not your goal. Use the full range if you need it, but don't feel obligated to do so."[18]

So far, so good—narrative-lyric balance and associative responses set you up well to meet the goal of the personal statement head on. In fact, the Common Application Board of Directors, in a prerelease memo posted on the Common Application website, explained that the Outreach Advisory Committee had recommended expanding the personal statement's word limit and revising the essay topics "to ensure that all applicants, regardless of background or access to counseling, would have the chance to tell their unique stories." The personal statement topics for the first edition of CA4 universally prompt applicants to share a moment or an experience—code words for personal narrative.

---

18. Dubbed CA4, it came into circulation for the 2013–14 admissions season. "New Essay Topics Announced," The Common Application website, February 5, 2013, www .commonapp.org/CommonApp/CA4.aspx.

However, a potential caveat for the detail-oriented applicant comes with this ideal format for telling personal narrative. Demand for a, well, common essay to all your prospective schools poses a fundamental problem. For those that require no supplemental statements, what you write for the personal statement will constitute the sum of your application writing. CA4 allows you to submit up to three revised drafts of your essay between submissions to various schools. This is allowed, though, with the understanding that changes will be minor or merely corrections, and that you are still submitting essentially the same essay to all your prospective schools.

However, prospective schools that require supplemental application essays force you to think differently about how the Common Application personal statement fits in with respective schools' supplemental statements. After all, how can a common personal statement have the same value or impact for one school that requires no supplemental writing as it does for a school that does require supplemental writing? And what if the story you want to tell for the Common Application is similar to the one you want to tell for a particular school's supplemental statement? Also, any two of your prospective Common Application schools will glean, beyond basic characteristics of a good student, different qualities from your writing and application at large.

For your prospective schools that use the Common Application, it makes sense first to organize all the schools' prompts side by side so that you can see where there are potential conflicts with the Common Application personal statement and opportunities to modify the same essay for two or more applications.[19] Next, consider drafting two or three essays that can be used to address associatively one of the Common Application prompts. Let your natural inclination to write about one event or another (of all your life's experiences so far) lead your choices

---

19. See Appendix 5: Organizational Charts for helpful organizational charts that I have my students use (see also Appendix 9: *Easy Being Green* Online for instructions on how to download free versions of these charts online). While they take some time to complete initially, they will save you considerable time and energy in the long run.

of topics, independent of how many prospective schools do or do not require supplemental writing in their respective applications. Once you have drafted two or three potential Common Application personal statements, then you might begin to consider which one of them will best meet all your schools' application requirements. This way, at least, you have narrowed down your choice of Common Application essay to just the few that you felt urged to write.

At this point in your high school career, admissions factors like GPA, standardized test scores, and teacher recommendations are either established, fairly consistent, or are out of your control. Two factors alone—the application essay and the interview—remain for you to define yourself as an applicant. And to get an admissions interview (with schools that require them), you must shape the application essay in a way that will appeal to all the schools you have in mind.

Strategically speaking, you can tailor a supplemental essay to address the broad categories of *volunteer work*, *work experience*, or *extracurricular activities* often considered in the admissions process. Other remaining admissions factors like *talent/ability*, *character/personal qualities*, *racial/ethnic status*, and *first-generation college student* could then be the focus of your main Common Application essay—once again, if you can wrap a solid narrative around it.

Altogether, required admissions writing allows an applicant to speak strategically to known admissions categories like those above, suggested by the College Board, and other criteria or personal qualities that are often advertised on universities' websites as factors they take into consideration in their admissions decisions.

APPENDIX 4

TIMELINES FOR APPLYING

Time Is on My Side

In an ideal world, rising seniors would begin the application process sometime in July. That sounds cruel, given that most high schools get out in mid- or late June, but it really is in your best interest to make a deliberate and controlled go at your applications over the course of several months. You can see that the admissions process is difficult and time consuming even if you plan ahead. While I love to see great results, I also love to see great process, and I strongly believe that the two are tightly intertwined.

Although the Common Application does not get released until August 1, you now have the tools to get started on brainstorming and drafting potential application essays and on researching prospective schools. Using the narrative techniques outlined in this book, you will likely write a fitting essay for one of the Common Application prompts before you even see them. If you are starting the application process after the start of your senior year but earlier than, say, late October, then modify this timeline to suit your situation. You can also condense this timeline if you want to move at a faster pace (see "I'm under the Gun" later in this appendix if you are really in a hurry). You may also modify this timeline if your school has an application process of its own to follow. Please note that this timeline is primarily concerned with the college applications proper. You may find that you also need to make considerations for other college-related hurdles like (re)taking the ACT or SAT and applying for scholarships and grants.

Mid-July

- Take an hour to write an essay on anything that comes to mind. Read a few essays a day from Part I of this book. Note models you like and start brainstorming ideas for your own essays (see Appendix 2: Strategies for Brainstorming Personal Material).
- Start or continue to make campus visits.
- Put together a student résumé. (Speak with your high school's guidance office or look up examples online.)
- Consider forming an essay writing group with friends who are also applying to college.

August

- Start or continue to make campus visits.
- Access the current Common Application starting August 1. Start checking for applications from schools that do not use the Common Application and for supplemental application materials from schools that do.
- Start filling out the Application-Essay Tracker Chart and Application Deadline Chart (see Appendix 5: Organizational Charts). Read Part II, especially sections that delve into explanations related to your favorite essays from Parts I and II, and draft at least one candidate for the Common Application personal statement.
- Get feedback on essays and make revisions.

September

- Start or continue to make campus visits.
- Prepare teacher recommendation materials (see Appendix 6: Teacher Recommendations).
- Solicit teacher recommendations by the end of September and be sure to give your recommenders at least a month to write their letters.
- Draft at least one more Common Application personal statement if you are not happy with your first essay or if you want another to choose.
- Get feedback on essays and make revisions.

October

- Start or continue to make campus visits and put together a tentative list of six to ten schools you're considering.
- Check in with recommenders according to the time frame you mentioned in your cover letters to them.
- Begin drafting application essays for schools that do not use the Common Application and for supplemental application materials from schools that do. Start with those that are due earliest.

November

- Early-admission and early-decision applications are due as early as November 1.
- Confirm submission of recommendations and send thank-you notes/gifts to your recommenders. Start drafting or modifying essays for regular-admission applications that are due next.
- Attend early-action/-decision interview(s) with alumni or campus officials and send thank-you cards (see Appendix 7: Interview with an Ivy League Interviewer).
- Revisit potential new teacher recommenders now that the semester is well under way.

- Consider mixing up recommenders for remaining schools if you think you can get a stronger letter of support from at least one and if any of your applications allows you to. If so, then repeat the process from September and October.
- If applicable, add new schools to your organizational charts and delete others that you are no longer considering.

December

- Continue drafting or modifying essays for regular-admission applications that are due next. Results for early action and early decision will begin arriving around the start of winter break.
- *If you have secured binding admission to the school of your choice, it is your moral obligation to contact the admissions offices of the schools you have applied to so far and ask them to remove your name from consideration. Do this for any school that you have no intention of attending now.*
- If you still have applications to complete at this point, the next round will likely be due December 31 or January 1.

January

- Continue drafting or modifying essays for regular-admission applications that are due this month.

February

- Some application deadlines are as late as February 15 (or later for schools with rolling admissions). Continue drafting or modifying essays for regular-admission applications that are due next.
- Complete the Free Application for Federal Student Aid (FAFSA).

March and April

- *Wait patiently. Do not contact admissions offices unless you have an important update to your application like a recent award, an improved test score, or a correction.*
- If you contact a school, follow the instructions on each school's admissions website *exactly*. All other contact puts your application at risk, plain and simple. Some admissions decisions could come by the end of March.
- Any schools that have placed you on a waiting list may ask that you briefly get in touch to indicate that you would still like to be considered for admission. Follow these directions closely and do not stray from them.
- Begin deliberating about your final decision. Consider making additional campus visits to schools that are still in contention. Some will invite you to a weekend event for admitted students.
- *Under no circumstances should you go online to bad-mouth schools to which you have not been accepted. This could come back to bite you.*

May and June

- Many schools to which you have been admitted will want a written commitment from you as early as May 1 and a deposit by a printed date.
- Even for schools that you won't be attending, be sure to let these admissions offices know your decision as soon as possible and no later than the deadline indicated in your acceptance materials—remember that you may very well be taking an admissions spot from someone on a waiting list.
- Let your recommenders, guidance counselor, and other mentors know about your final decision. They will be eager to hear and to share in your excitement.

I'm under the Gun

If the unabridged timeline makes you shiver, if you are feeling way too overwhelmed by the application process, or if you are just beginning to realize how much is involved in applying to college, then use the following condensed timeline to help you get your bearings. Even if you are working on a tighter schedule than what is suggested here, you can modify it to meet your needs. Or you can find a balance between these two suggested timelines. Odds are that you will be able to catch up by December, so this timeline is abridged for the summer and fall only. (And, yes, you are still going to college.)

Late October/Early November

- Solicit your teacher recommendations ASAP. Decide on at least three schools to which you want to apply and get going on the school(s) with the earliest deadline(s). What type of prompts(s) does it give you?
- Read a couple of essays from each chapter in Part I of this book and zero in on a few that seem to fit the bill. Note model essays in this book that you like and start brainstorming ideas for your own essay (see Appendix 2: Strategies for Brainstorming Personal Material).
- Turn to the corresponding chapters and sections in Part II to get a sense for how to write an essay in the mold of the ones you admire.
- Try to visit a school in your area to which you will be applying.
- If you have the time, put together a student résumé. (Speak with your high school's guidance office or look up examples online.)
- Follow up with your recommenders by the end of November (but remember that a month is a courteous amount of time to give them to write their letters).
- Draft your Common Application personal statement.
- Get feedback on essays and make revisions (see Part II for suggestions).

November

- Early-admission and early-decision applications are due as early as November 1. Confirm submission of recommendations and send thank-you notes/gifts to your recommenders.
- Start drafting or modifying essays for regular-admission applications that are due next.
- Attend early-action/-decision interview(s) with alumni or campus officials and send thank-you cards (see Appendix 7: Interview with an Ivy League Interviewer).
- If applicable, add new schools to your organizational charts and delete others that you are no longer considering.

December

- Continue drafting or modifying essays for regular-admission applications that are due next. Results for early action and early decision will begin arriving around the start of winter break.
- *If you have secured admission to the school of your choice, it is your moral obligation to contact the admissions offices of the schools you have applied to so far and ask them to remove your name from consideration. Do this for any school that you have no intention of attending now.*
- If you still have applications to complete at this point, the next round will likely be due December 31 or January 1.

January

- Continue drafting or modifying essays for regular-admission applications that are due this month.

February

- Some application deadlines are as late as February 15 (or later for schools with rolling admissions). Continue drafting or modifying essays for regular-admission applications that are due next.
- Complete the Free Application for Federal Student Aid (FAFSA).

March and April

- *Wait patiently. Do not contact admissions offices unless you have an important update to your application like an award, an improved test score, or a correction.* If you must contact a school, follow the instructions on each school's admissions website *exactly.* All other contact puts your application at risk, plain and simple. Some admissions decisions could come by the end of March.
- Any schools that have placed you on a waiting list may ask that you briefly get in touch to indicate that you would still like to be considered for admission. Follow these directions closely and do not stray from them.
- Begin deliberating about your final decision. Consider making additional campus visits to schools that are still in contention. Some will invite you to a weekend event for admitted students.
- *Under no circumstances should you go online to bad-mouth schools to which you have not been accepted. This could come back to bite you.*

May and June

- Many schools to which you have been admitted will want a written commitment from you as early as May 1 and a deposit by a printed date. Even for schools that you won't be attending, be sure to let these admissions offices know your decision as soon as possible and no later than the deadline indicated in your acceptance materials—remember that you may very well be taking an admissions spot from someone on a waiting list.

- Let your recommenders, guidance counselor, and other mentors know about your final decision. They will be eager to hear and to share in your excitement.

APPENDIX 5

ORGANIZATIONAL CHARTS

FOLLOWING ARE TWO CHARTS that will help you keep organized throughout the application process. See Appendix 9: *Easy Being Green* Online for information about downloading your own copies of these charts.

Application Deadline Chart

Fill in the following chart as you learn the application requirements for your prospective schools. With a bit of planning, you could be able to use or modify a few essays for all your schools.

School				
Uses Common Application (Y/N)				

Total no. of essays for this school (approx. 500 words)				
Summary of main prompt(s) w/ word count				
Other schools this essay(s) can be used/ modified for				
Application deadline				
My target date for submission				

No. of applications _____/ Total no. of essays _____/
Total no. of shorter prompts _____

Application-Essay Tracker

Look up applications for colleges and then list the number of writing components and lengths. Then use the following chart to compare similarities between college prompts. Which could potentially be answered with the same essay or a variation of it?

College/ University	Uses the Common Application?	Summary of college-specific personal essay prompt(s) and length(s)	Application deadline

APPENDIX 6

TEACHER RECOMMENDATIONS

C LEARLY, STUDENTS HAVE TO work harder these days to stand out from the applicant field. Strategies on topically organizing your essays can help create an impression of you as an applicant that answers a university's stated admission factors, and your choice of prospective schools will correlate to your extracurricular, testing, and academic achievements. Beyond these student-controlled factors lies the last portion of the paper applications—teacher recommendations, which represent a candid, comparative look at you as a student, person, and member of your school community.

If you go to a high school that is like my alma mater (at least at the time of my graduation), there is no formal procedure to secure a teacher's recommendation. You generally need letters from three different teachers. Perhaps because of the heightened competitiveness of admissions these days (or perhaps some schools always did and some never have), many high school guidance departments have formal— even in-depth—procedures for securing letters of recommendation from teachers, which is excellent for a number of reasons I'll touch on.

A controlled approach to securing teacher recommendations falls in line with the application strategies discussed in Appendix 3: Matching Essays with Applications. You the student do not write these letters, but there are measures you can take to increase the odds that your teachers' letters of recommendation will not only be strong but that they will also round out the image that you are seeking to present to your prospective schools. Following is a thorough set of forms that both student and parents submit to recommending teachers at Biotechnology High School (BTHS), a nationally recognized magnet school in Freehold, New Jersey. After these forms are a few simple tips to keep in mind when securing teacher recommendations. Remember, if there are parts of this packet that aren't useful to you, you can modify this example to create your own packet of forms. See Appendix 9: *Easy Being Green* Online for information about downloading your own copies of this packet.

BTHS Faculty-Teacher Recommendation Request

1. Please enter your full name:

2. Activities/course(s) taken with faculty member:

3. Why have you requested this faculty member to write a recommendation for you? And what did you like best about the class/course you took with them?

4. How has this class/activity/faculty member helped you grow as a student? As an individual?

5. What three adjectives/descriptive phrases best define you and why?

6. What, so far in your life, has been your greatest accomplishment/triumph? Of which are you most proud?

7. What is your intended course of study/major? Career choice? If not 100 percent sure, please indicate your thoughts at this point.

8. What colleges/universities are your top three choices?

BTHS Parent Brag Sheet

We have seen your children grow and mature for a short time while they have been students at BTHS, but you are the best resource to give a complete picture. Please answer the following questions and return this form to the guidance office. If appropriate, some of this information may be included in the letter of recommendation.

1. Over the past three years, what outstanding accomplishments has your child achieved?

2. In what area has your child shown the most development and growth over the past three years?

3. What outstanding personality traits do you see in your child?

4. What five adjectives would you use to describe your child?

5. Are there any unusual or personal circumstances that have affected your child's education or personal experiences?

Parent Signature _____

Student Signature _____

BTHS Student Activity Report

Please list all BTHS sponsored clubs, societies, awards/recognition, and activities you were involved in or a member of while a student at BTHS (all input must be typed). The objective of this report is to begin collecting BTHS school activities on all of our students that will be added to their official BTHS transcript. Listed activities can only include items that were observable by a BTHS staff member. These items will be added to your résumé, which will be packaged with your transcript for college admissions.

Name: _____ Grade: _____

A. Clubs   Member/Office (Title)   Dates

_____

_____

_____

_____

_____

B. Activities   Dates
(Evening of the Arts, Freshmen Orientation, Open House Committee, Girls' Night Out, etc.)

_____

_____

_____

_____

_____

_____

C. Awards/Recognition
(Example: NHS, National Merit Finalist, etc.)

_____

_____

_____

_____

_____

_____

In addition to the Faculty-Teacher Recommendation Request, the Parent Brag Sheet, and the Student Activity Report, BTHS students include _formal_ letters of request to their teachers and can also submit formal résumés that include both school- and nonschool-related experiences and activities (a quick search online will provide examples).

It takes a lot of work to put together these request packets, but schools like Biotechnology High that put their students through the paces are doing them a huge favor. Even if your school does not have (such) a formal process for requesting recommendations, you should make up a packet of your own using the BTHS forms here as models (or by browsing online). A few tips for securing teacher recommendations:

- Complete your request packet in the summer. If you have any solid drafts of your personal statement, consider including them in the packet.
- Select three teachers who will uniformly give you positive and enthusiastic reviews. One glowing report out of three can look like the exception to admissions personnel.
- Your three recommenders should teach core subjects like math, science, and English, especially if you plan to declare your major in a related field. Your main concern, again, is securing uniformly positive letters. If you have done well in AP, IB, or honors classes, then approach these teachers for recommendations.
- You can consider approaching a subject teacher (foreign language, art, and other electives) if the subject matter is central to the presentation of your application, if you have extracurricular experience or accomplishments in the field, or if you plan on declaring that field as a course of study on your applications.
- If your school does not have a formal procedure for requesting recommendations, then give your prospective recommenders notice about what you plan to do and why. This way, they will not feel overwhelmed when you hand over your materials.[20]
- Contact your prospective recommenders early—not during the hectic first week of school, but by the end of September. As soon as they agree, you will have your formal request packet ready to hand over.
- Request in your cover letter a due date that is at least two weeks ahead of the date you plan to submit your earliest applications.
- In your letters, make gentle mention that you will follow up with your teachers as the due date approaches. Since you have allowed

---

20. You can cite the benefits of doing so to bolster your case for a formal request to your recommenders.

yourself a two-week cushion, there is no reason to panic or to hassle your teachers if they do not submit your letters right on time.

- Once you are certain that your teachers have submitted their recommendations, write them each a formal thank-you note or give a small gift in recognition of their support.
- Keep your recommenders posted on your admissions news and be sure to tell them in the spring which school you plan to attend. They will feel gratified by your success and appreciated for having backed you during this process.

There are benefits to following formal guidelines for requesting recommendations, even if your high school does not have any:

- You will look professional, organized, and responsible to your recommenders, which will carry over into their assessment of you on paper. They can speak to your character and personal traits—evidence of which is often an admissions factor—without your having to do so directly.
- Your formal request packet will give recommenders a direct, concrete point of reference. Often enough, if recommenders agree with your self-assessments or find them helpful, they will do you the favor of paraphrasing your writing in their letters.
- Your recommenders will gain a more holistic picture of you beyond your interaction with them in the classroom. It can be exciting for a teacher to learn about the talents, interests, and successes of a student they "know."
- A formal request packet gives you the opportunity to address past grades with your recommender and to help him/her contextualize them in a narrative about your improvement.
- If you have successfully chosen three teachers who will all cheerlead for you, they will each want to give you the best recommendation that they can—and the best recommendation is the recommendation that you need. A deliberate request packet can help ensure that these are the letters that you get.

INTERVIEW WITH AN
IVY LEAGUE INTERVIEWER

BELOW ARE SOME THOUGHTS offered by an Ivy League alumna and admissions interviewer.

What do you recall about your admissions interview as a high school senior? What about it do you think helped you gain your interviewer's support for admission?

I had at least five college interviews. The two most memorable were those for my top pick (for which I was wait-listed and ultimately rejected) and for the school I attended. The interviewers in both these cases were less intimidating than others had been, and I'm sure this positively affected my performance. Both of these women also lived closer to where I grew up than the other interviewers did and perhaps had a better grasp of where I was coming from. Nonetheless, I doubt my performance was stellar in either of these, as I wasn't always the most confident or engaging teenager!

When you look back on your expectations of this university, how do you think the school panned out as an appropriate selection for you? How were your expectations left unmet, or in which ways do you think the university was not a good fit for you?

The school I attended is a prestigious one, but it was not my first choice. In the end, I can't really imagine having gone anywhere else. Sure, there are many students who are unhappy and decide to transfer at every school, but I think there's a lot to be said for the ways in which schools—and, hopefully, students—choose each other with an eye toward good fit. I'm not sure what my university had in mind for me when it admitted me—probably not what I ended up doing—but I made use of what was available to me and forged a unique career path.

Can you please elaborate a little more on that term *good fit*? We hear it so often these days as a premise for acceptance and rejection—not just in admissions. What does this mean to you?
I think "fit" is important to think about as an applicant but, importantly, applicants should recognize that fit is a two-way street. You're looking for something from your favored institutions, and they're looking for something from their applicants. That makes it all sound so self-interested, but I don't see it so much that way. Rather, the institution may have particular goals in mind—programs they're hoping to build or regions they're hoping to pull more students from. As an applicant, you can't know all this, and that's okay. But you need to do your part by asking questions—through your own research or of your interviewer—about how the institution will meet your needs. If you want to major in public policy, and that's not something offered by one institution, well, maybe you shouldn't apply there. Most important, again, is to recognize that fit is, in some ways, out of your control, and I think that can be liberating for anxiety-ridden applicants. You want to apply to the places that suit your needs the best but also accept the possibility that the institution may not feel the same about you as you do about it. Be a strong candidate and apply to places that make sense to you; follow your instincts but confirm them with thorough research.

Why did you decide to volunteer as an admissions interviewer for your alma mater?
Frankly, I was a graduate student with no money to donate to my alma

mater, but I did want to do something to stay involved in the alumni community. I know that my admission to my undergraduate institution was a crucial turning point in my life; it opened doors for me that I wouldn't have had access to otherwise. I was interested in meeting students who might be in similar positions. Part of my career as a qualitative social scientist is to talk to people and hear their stories. One of the challenges of this work is trying to capture the richness of people's experiences on paper; I know that lots of applicants struggle to do this on their college applications, and I liked the idea of being a liaison of sorts, to help translate their real selves, through my interview reports.

Why have you decided to share with readers anonymously and without naming your institution?
First and foremost, I am not speaking as an official representative of my institution, so I don't see it as appropriate to speak on its behalf. Second, revealing my name and the name of my institution might violate the privacy of the students I have interviewed, and I have no desire to do that. Also, the admissions process is fluid. The needs of institutions, including my own, are always changing, and I make no claims to know what, in a very specific sense, my institution is looking for in any given year. (A cello player, for example? I have no idea!) However, I do have a general understanding of how interviews fit into the process and what interviews can and cannot do for you as an applicant.

Has your work as an interviewer given you insight on college admissions? What have you learned about the admissions process from your time as an applicant to your time as an alumna involved with applicants?
I've learned that interviews are a small but powerful part of the admissions process. A good interview is not going to compensate for lackluster credentials, but it can assuage minor doubts and report exceptional charisma, enthusiasm, and warmth. It's also an opportunity for applicants to reveal meaningful parts of themselves that don't fit anywhere

else in the application process, maybe an opportunity to explain a gap or a challenge. Importantly, the interview gives applicants a chance to convince the institution of interest in ways that go behind the trite "It's my dream school" claims on written materials.

What qualities do you look for in an applicant? Why are these qualities important in recommending an applicant for admission?
I look for students who demonstrate intellectual curiosity, who are focused but not self-limiting. I don't look for well-rounded students in the formulaic sense—*I play a sport, volunteer, and love science*—but rather a complex individual who has real and genuinely diverse interests, no matter how seemingly trivial or quirky. I am sure most college graduates can recall peers whose paths were so determined that they failed to take advantage of even a fraction of the opportunities presented by their institutions and the surrounding communities. I hope my institution admits students who will make the most of the place, in a broad sense.

Importantly—and I can't tell you how often applicants do not do this—they should express real interest in and knowledge of the institution. If they live within a day's drive, they should have visited prior to the interview. If they haven't, they should have a very good reason for not having done that. Most colleges are still physical places with campuses that largely define the experiences students have. Applicants can rarely convince me of their interest without having seen the place and imagined themselves there.

What do you expect an applicant to know about the university? Should s/he know "everything"?
I don't have unrealistic expectations. I know that most students are applying to at least a half-dozen schools, each of which has unique curricula. However, whether it's your first choice or your last, my institution might be the only one that admits you, so don't waste an opportunity to do well on the interview. Take a few hours to browse the college's

website, look at the general education or core requirements, and look at the trajectories for the majors or programs that most interest you. You should be able to tell your interviewer what makes this school uniquely suited to your goals, and that's not a one-sentence, one-size-fits-all response like "They offer a biology major."

Do you have any other turn-offs as an interviewer?

Don't abandon basic courtesy. I know your senior year of high school is a busy one, but respond to emails and phone messages from interviewers. While interviews are not required for admission to most institutions, it doesn't look good if you miss an opportunity to have one. Likewise, arrive on time, don't dress too casually, and send a thank-you email or card. A thank-you note is your last opportunity to impress me, and it's something you should do even if you have no interest in my institution anymore.

I'm also shocked when applicants don't ask me any questions, especially if they don't know anyone else who has attended my university. This is a place where you'll be spending four years; if I were an applicant again, I'd want to know what life was like on campus, whether faculty were receptive to undergraduates, and what kinds of things graduates ended up doing next.

Perhaps the most generic advice to applicants is to "be yourself" during the interview. What does this advice mean to you, and how can you tell if an applicant is not acting naturally? Is this different from simply being nervous?

Nervousness is natural. Some students are very poised—and that's wonderful—but I don't expect that from everyone. Find balance between confidence and humility. Don't throw yourself under the bus, but be up front about glaring weaknesses in your application. Don't pretend to have interests that you don't. If you're interested in something but have never pursued it, tell me why my institution is good place for you to do that. I'm as impressed by students who have things on the horizon—things they want to try or learn—as I am by students who have already done those things.

Your alma mater is obviously a highly selective school. Does a strong recommendation from you, the interviewer, automatically result in a student's acceptance? Have there been students you were surprised not to see accepted?

The interview is a small part of the application process, and I think it is a make-or-break factor in only a small number of cases. I have seen a couple of students who impressed me get wait-listed or rejected, but for the most part, I've found that the best interviewees are often the ones who are accepted. Their excellent interviews didn't hurt, I'm sure, but I imagine their applications were far more important in their acceptances. Of course, when we talk about highly selective schools, we have to keep in mind that lots of bright, capable students get rejected. So when I say "the best interviewees," I'm really talking about a minority of those I interview; many other interviewees were quite wonderful. I probably wouldn't have been in the "best" category when I was accepted by my alma mater, but the competition has intensified since then. I urge students to do the best they can do in the interview but also to trust that if they cover their bases by applying to enough schools for which they are good fits, they will find a place where they are happy.

The Ivy League is the biggest name in the American university system—in the world, for that matter. Do you ever get the impression that students are set on Ivy League schools solely for the names? What advice do you have for students who are competitive applicants but who might not have concrete reasons for applying to an Ivy League school?

Again, students need to do the research on individual institutions. I suspect that most interviewers are attuned to how personalized applicants' interests in institutions are. All of the Ivies are different. If you don't want to be in an introductory lecture course of one hundred students, you can rule out a number of the Ivies. There are also many highly selective, small schools with excellent faculty and strong alumni networks, and there are many wonderful public institutions that offer equally excellent faculty at a fraction of the cost of private schools. My institution offered me many benefits, and while I can't imagine having gone anywhere else, realistically, I would have probably done just fine at a number of other colleges.

Any other reflections or advice for college hopefuls?

I understand the tendency to get one's hopes pinned on one institution or another—I know I did. Take it from someone who was quite pleased with her second choice (or maybe third or fourth; I can't remember— and that, in and of itself, says something): very few people are still hung up on where they didn't get admitted after their first year of college. It's important to remember that you can have an impact wherever you go to school.

INTERVIEW WITH A STANFORD STUDENT-ATHLETE ALUMNUS

Nɪᴄᴋ Eʟʟɪs ᴀᴛᴛᴇɴᴅᴇᴅ Sᴛᴀɴꜰᴏʀᴅ University (1998–2002), where he helped win two NCAA Division I championships as the goalie for the men's water polo team. In addition to serving as team captain, he was a four-time Stanford Scholar Athlete and the Block S Award recipient as the university's most outstanding male athlete in the junior class, among other honors. He continues to play competitively and internationally.

For those who are not familiar with water polo as a sport or as subculture, help readers understand its prevalence on the West Coast and the level of competition in the Pac-12.
Much like lacrosse is well recognized on the East Coast, water polo is most popular on the West Coast. The sport began in England in the mid-nineteenth century, and today the best teams in the world play only a few hundred miles farther east: Hungary, Italy, and Spain are among the very best, though almost every European country has a competitive team. Globally, water polo is recognized as one of (often *the*) most demanding sports in the world. Think wrestling, in the water, with a ball flying at you and other players haranguing you.

In California—the hotbed of USA water polo, where more than 90 percent of our Olympic athletes come from—the sport has captured the imagination of tens of thousands of young men and women, most of whom begin playing in middle school or high school. The most successful youth athletes often earn scholarships to top-tier universities (this was my path) and, even for those who don't play in college, many continue to compete with masters' teams (as I do today).

Water polo has changed my life. The camaraderie, athletic and intellectual challenges, and international popularity of the sport have kept me engaged and traveling around the world for nearly twenty-five years. I've played, coached, mentored, refereed, and fund-raised, and continue to fall in love with the people, places, and beauty of the sport.

Describe your recruitment experience out of high school. When did you know you might succeed at the college level and in Division I competition in particular? What other schools were you seriously considering, and what sealed your decision to attend and play for Stanford?

I was fortunate to begin playing polo early, and began competing with all-star teams when I was thirteen. Shortly after that (at about fifteen), I started to get signals from college coaches that they'd be interested in speaking with me when I became eligible. For the most part, these were just passing comments made to me or my parents, and my high school coaches often reaffirmed that college coaches were asking about eligibility (to be clear, it was all by the book—no recruiting violations in my story).

When the time came, I took recruiting trips to five colleges, though not all were Division I schools. I paid visits to Harvard and MIT, both schools that had emerging programs and great academics, but I decided that I wanted the best of both worlds. My decision was really made before I visited Stanford, and confirmed once I met the team. Their attitudes, goals in life, and vibe resonated with me, and confirmed that I would be happiest at Stanford. Yes, we had a great time going to basketball games, hanging at frat parties, and visiting classes, but it really came down to the students for me—these will be your friends for life and, though professors and parties will make an impression, nothing endures like good friendships.

Could you speculate on the role athletic prowess played in your admission to Stanford?

I don't think I would have been admitted to Harvard or Stanford without athletics—it was a centerpiece of my value proposition for each school and, equally important, a key piece of the experience I wanted to have in college. My dream was to win an NCAA championship, so sports were never a question for me or a way to "game" the admissions process. It was just part and parcel of who I was. At the end of the day, I do believe the admissions office looks at the whole applicant—beyond being an athlete. At that time, I had a strong sense of what I wanted to do with my life (social entrepreneurship), and to this day, I believe that clarity of purpose had a major impact on the admissions committee's perception of me as someone with good goals, strong values, and a lifelong commitment to public-benefit work that they could support.

I'd encourage every applicant to be honest and thoughtful about what they want out of a particular university—they are each different, and will impact where your life leads you.

What did you write about for your application essay(s)? How did your essay compliment your athletic profile and value proposition?

I recall writing one essay about a childhood babysitter, Mrs. Janet, who strongly influenced my life. Mrs. Janet was exceptional in showing compassion to others, and at an early age, that made an indelible mark on my own values: to always be generous to others and to listen before you speak.

When writing to an admissions committee, I'd encourage athletes to highlight their most noble personal values—be they sportsmanship, teamwork, or something else entirely—and give the committee a sense of who you are apart from athletics. These days, it's about the "whole package," which extends beyond academics and athletics, and into what drives you personally and what your life ambitions are. Admittedly, that can be a tall order when you're eighteen, but take the time to give it some thought, and honestly share what comes out of those reflections.

How might students determine whether Division I, II, or III athletics would be the best choice for them?
It really comes down to finding your tribe of people. If those folks are in DI or DIII schools, then that's your tribe and you should trust your gut. There's no right choice. Practically speaking, DI schools offer a high-pressure athletic environment where you train harder and have more attention (press, social, alumni) focused on you but, at the end of the day, if you're with friends and having a great time, these things turn out to be what matters least in defining your experience.

What advice do you have to prospective recruits? How should they go about communicating with a coach? Beyond athletics, what is a coach looking for in a potential recruit?
First, observe the recruiting rules. Beyond that, be proactive about reaching out to coaches and expressing your interest in playing for their schools. Send an email, make a phone call, write a letter—most coaches are incredibly honest and professional and will respond quickly, which helps you figure out where you've got the best chance of playing. As far as what coaches look for, that varies by coach. Generally speaking, work ethic and leadership potential are always in high demand. Role players are also invaluable for some teams—just be honest about who you are and what you have to offer, and the coach will help guide you through the process.

What advice can you offer to walk-ons? For example, do you think hopes of walking onto a team should be a big factor in attending a college?
Each university has a different walk-on policy. At Stanford, we let

anyone come out, but made cuts within the first two or three days. At Berkeley, they never cut anyone, and had over sixty people on the team while I was competing against them. The benefit for Berkeley was that this grew the membership and fan base, and also created intense competition for the top slots. The flipside is that you have to have incredibly committed coaches to run a 24/7 program like that. If being a walk-on is important to you, then identify a school that encourages them, and then give it your best shot. This is where early and clear communication with a potential coach will help you make the right decision.

Can you please quantify the commitment in terms of weekly hours dedicated to practicing, training, and traveling and how it might differ from sport to sport?
There are NCAA regulations that limit total training hours in any one week, but there are additional hours athletes spend traveling to and from these events. You can probably expect your preseason and in-season routines to take three to five hours per day, six days a week.

What strategies did you use to balance the demands of training, traveling, being with family and friends, and studying?
Travel was never an issue—trips were often short (water polo is unique in that we never had to go further than a three-hour drive or a two-hour flight because the best competition is on the West Coast), and when we had to miss class (rarely), our professors were accommodating.

In terms of balancing the responsibilities, most guys on the team held it together really well. And if we were struggling in school (I had a tough time in my freshman-year Italian course), we asked for help—in my case, my professor committed to spending an extra hour a week with me to ensure I developed a good grasp of the language (*grazie mille*, Giovanni!). In short, it's one of the hardest challenges of adjusting to college life—controlling your own schedule can be daunting, but if you have good habits and a good social-support structure, you typically figure it out pretty quickly.

I actually had my best academic quarters while water-polo was in-season, largely because it forced me to manage my time well. In the winter and spring quarters, I had a tougher time keeping up with course demands because I had so much free time and ended up partying a bit too much.

Family was another key component of doing well at school—I talked with my parents weekly, sometimes daily, which helped me stay focused and slowly break the bond from home life. Stanford was great in that it felt like home from day one, but there's still a gnawing feeling we all wrestle with when we leave home for the first (and typically last) time. Family makes the difference—draw on them as you need to. They want to see you succeed and will typically do anything they can to help, even if it's as simple as taking your phone call.

To the best of your knowledge, how did your student-athlete experience at Stanford compare with those of friends at other schools? Is there a great difference in what is required of student-athletes in different sports at Stanford?

Stanford's different—there's no denying it. The legacy of sportsmanship at the school is second to none, and competing on one of the school teams is one of the highest honors a college kid can earn. In terms of the requirements for each sport, one thing that's funny about Stanford is that I don't believe there's a difference in the commitment the student-athletes make to any one sport. Case in point, our men's and women's ultimate Frisbee teams were among the best in the nation—even though they were (and still are) club sports; they worked their tails off every day as if a Division I championship was on the line. The desire to win at Stanford permeates every facet of school life, particularly in the classroom and on the field. In that regard, Stanford is unique—it's a culture of winning and a commitment to self-improvement, and the bar gets raised every year.

Did you know any athletes who were recruited at Stanford but who did not play all four years of their college careers? What are a few reasons these athletes didn't continue in their sports?
Yes, many. Most either fell in love with their studies or fell out of love with water polo. Every one of them did phenomenally well in school and, in retrospect, made the right decision for him- or herself. The message here is that we all walk our own path in life and, though decisions like this are hard at the time, if done with good intention and forethought, they often turn out for the best.

What was your major? What are doing now professionally and what your plans for the future? Do you see a direct correlation between your major and your professional trajectory?
I studied human-computer interaction (a mix of computer science and psychology) at Stanford, and then studied technology policy at the London School of Economics. Both degrees were heavy on systems thinking, and gave me a great framework for solving complex problems. When I left school, I purposely sought out jobs that would help me build a skill set that would make me a strong business leader. I first worked in public finance, where I learned how public taxes are approved, collected, and then appropriated for financing public infrastructure (schools, parks, etc.). Phenomenal experience that schooled me in economics, markets, and public policy. Later, as an entrepreneur, I continued to learn about fund-raising, sales, hiring, firing (no fun), managing teams, and growing a business. I've also overseen a couple business failures—you truly do learn more from failure than success.

Going forward, I plan to stay focused on public-benefit work in the private sector. It's a broad lens that gives me the freedom to work in a multitude of industries, while ensuring that my energy is ultimately directed to the greater good.

How has Stanford's tight alumni network helped you or allowed you to help others? Are you active in the alumni network?

It's been instrumental—the alumni network at Stanford is unparalleled (maybe Harvard competes, from what I have heard). It's honestly one of the best parts about going to school at Stanford—the community is just on fire. I got my first job from an alumnus (who continues to be a key mentor) and, at every stage, the Stanford network has been key to my success. My wish is that every kid could attend Stanford and benefit from the experience the same way that I have.

I actively mentor current students and recent graduates—it's a great part of my life. The kids are just getting smarter, and it's an honor to help them realize their dreams.

I've also been deeply involved in fund-raising. I co-chaired my five- and ten-year reunions, and continue to make donations every year because I believe that every kid should have an opportunity to attend Stanford, regardless of household income.

APPENDIX 9

EASY BEING GREEN ONLINE

F OR HELPFUL MATERIALS, VISIT www.beinggreenbook.com, the book's complementary website. There you will find:.

- Downloadable Application-Essay Tracker Chart and Application-Deadlines Chart
- Downloadable Biotechnology High School (BTHS) Faculty-Teacher Recommendation Request packet
- Access to articles on college applications, funding, costs, athletics, and trends
- Resources on personal essays and memoirs

Sources Used

Baldwin, James. "Notes of a Native Son." In *The Best American Essays of the Century*, edited by Joyce Carol Oates and Robert Atwan, 220–38. The Best American Series. New York: Houghton Mifflin, 2000.

Barrett, Andrea. "The Sea of Information." In *The Best American Essays 2005*, edited by Susan Orlean and Robert Atwan, 9–20. The Best American Series. New York: Houghton Mifflin, 2005.

Conway, Jill Ker. "Points of Departure." In *Inventing the Truth: The Art and Craft of Memoir*, edited by William Zinsser, 41–59. New York: Mariner, 1998.

Dillard, Annie. "To Fashion a Text." In *Inventing the Truth: The Art and Craft of Memoir*, edited by William Zinsser, 141–61. New York: Mariner, 1998.

Kingston, Maxine Hong. "No Name Woman." In *The Best American Essays of the Century*, edited by Joyce Carol Oates and Robert Atwan, 383–94. The Best American Series. New York: Houghton Mifflin, 2000.

"New Essay Topics Announced." The Common Application. www
.commonapp.org/CommonApp/CA4.aspx.

Sondheim, Stephen. "Putting It Together." *Sunday in the Park with
George*. CD. Warner/Chappell Music, 2000.

Star Wars. Directed by George Lucas. Film. Lucasfilm, 1977.

About the Contributors

Brianna B. moved to the small town of Gilmanton, New Hampshire, when she was in the third grade. After graduating from Gilford High School with high honors in the top 5 percent of her class, she went on to become a freshman at Keene State College in the fall of 2013. On top of her challenging honors and AP course load at school, she still managed to maintain a steady job at Market Basket since 2009 and worked upward of forty hours each week. At Keene, Brianna plans to major in biology and premed in hopes of someday entering the medical field.

Mary R. Becker is from northeastern Massachusetts. She grew up in a small rural town. She loves to go to the beach (no matter what time of year). She has enrolled in Mount Holyoke College. Mary currently works in the halal/kosher dining hall. In the past, she worked in a greenhouse. In her "spare time," Mary likes to read and garden. She also enjoys art. Mary will graduate in 2017. Her plans for the future include a major in international relations, joining the Peace Corps, and earning at least her master's degree.

Lauren Beriont grew up on the coast of New Jersey, attending Rumson-Fair Haven public schools. After high school graduation, she moved out to Ann Arbor, Michigan, to pursue an undergraduate degree in environmental sciences at the University of Michigan. Lauren, prompted by her completion of a bachelor's in sciences and inspired by the knowledge she amassed over four years, moved out to Madison, Wisconsin, to put her degree to use. She currently lives in Madison and is pursuing a career confronting socio-environmental issues. In her free time, you can find her contemplating at the edge of one of Madison's lakes or experimenting with new home-brew recipes.

Chris C. is from Old Bridge, New Jersey. He graduated from Old Bridge High School, where he was ranked in the top 5 percent of his class. During high school, Chris participated in many extracurricular activities, such as peer leadership, which offered him interaction with the student population of the school. He played baseball all four years and continues to play sports for fun while at Rutgers University, where he is majoring in mechanical engineering. After graduation, he hopes to obtain a job at an engineering firm in the New York area.

H. Charles grew up—mostly—in woodsy New Hampshire, where he had ample time to develop a love for hiking and reading. He graduated from Amherst College in Massachusetts with a religion major and moved to Kyoto, Japan, as a teaching fellow at Doshisha University. In Kyoto, he practiced the Japanese tea ceremony and embraced twentieth-century Japanese literature. He is currently applying to graduate programs in East Asian concentrations and trying to make a living in Boston working in the food and conservation industries. Someday he'd like to own a house with a wood stove so he can once again feel the happy heft of an ax in his hands.

Amanda Chiodo hails from Old Bridge, New Jersey, and currently attends The Ohio State University. She is a first-year student and plans to graduate in 2017. She is majoring in hospitality management and seeking a minor in business. Having an interest in international affairs, she wants to travel the world through her work. After graduation, she aspires to work in another country for a well-known resort. Then, after living abroad for a few years, she plans to return to the United States and get involved with managing events for sports teams or managing the affairs of a team for when they travel. She looks forward to all the different opportunities that her career will bring her.

Carly David was raised in Concord, New Hampshire, and attended the St. Paul's School Advanced Studies Program, where she wrote the essay attributed to her in this book. She graduated from Lafayette College in Easton, Pennsylvania, in 2013 with a bachelor of science in biology and a minor in health and life science. Having worked for the Office of Admissions and the Department of Biology at Lafayette, Carly is pursuing a career in research and she hopes to one day earn her master's in public health. Her essay, "Adella," is dedicated to the loving memory of Adella Freo (1900–2010)—a great-grandmother who, throughout her long life, taught her entire family to laugh and enjoy the simple things.

Nicholas Dube was raised in Litchfield, New Hampshire, and graduated from Harvard College in 2012, where he majored in history and classics. He enjoys rowing on the Charles River, traveling throughout Europe, and studying *The Divine Comedy*. He has had the privilege of performing plays in the United States and Italy, where he holds dual citizenship. One of his most rewarding experiences has been teaching and mentoring elementary school children. After graduating from college, Nicholas worked for one year as a paralegal at an international law firm in Washington, DC. He plans to become a lawyer and is currently pursuing this goal at Harvard Law School.

Emily R. Fernandes is currently a graduate student pursuing a degree in electrical engineering at Rensselaer Polytechnic Institute. She is honored to be a part of this project.

D. G. is from Colts Neck, New Jersey, and currently attends Brown

University. He graduated from Biotechnology High School in Freehold, New Jersey, and plans to pursue a major in biochemistry. His hobbies include music (piano and saxophone), running, and crossword puzzles. He plans to become a scientific researcher and/or doctor.

Lauren G. is from New Jersey. She currently attends Boston University and will be graduating in 2017. Lauren is enrolled in the school of management and is planning on majoring in international business.

Eliza Gettel is from New Hampshire and graduated from Bishop Guertin High School (2008) in Nashua. For college, she attended College of the Holy Cross in Worcester, Massachusetts, on a full-tuition scholarship to study classics. During her undergraduate career, she studied and worked on archaeological projects in Italy, Greece, and Jordan. She graduated *summa cum laude* in spring 2012 and won a Fulbright award to study for her master's in social archaeology in the UK at the University of Southampton. In fall 2013, she returned to the United States to start her PhD in ancient history at Harvard University. She plans to become a professor of Greek and Roman history.

Michael H. is a graduate student at the University of New Hampshire in the MAT program. As an undergrad, he studied English teaching, women's studies, and studio art, as well as practiced journalism and social change theater. Currently, he is an intern teacher at a public high school in New Hampshire. With his teaching and residence life experience with pre-K, middle, and high school students in New Hampshire and North Carolina, he plans to make a career as a high school English teacher and antiviolence educator.

Ian M. Jesset lives in Moscow, Russia, where he teaches English as a foreign language. He attended the University of Notre Dame and graduated in 2012 with a degree in mathematics and an interest in poetry.

G. K. was born and raised in Queens, New York, and graduated from Benjamin N. Cardozo High School in 2013. She was accepted into Swarthmore College, where she started in the fall of 2013. She plans to major in biochemistry and minor in history. Expecting to graduate during the summer of 2017, she plans to attend medical school. During her free time, she likes to listen to Korean music and talk with her friends. She also enjoys watching movies as well as spending time with her family.

Kayleigh Kangas is a 2013 graduate of the University of Connecticut. As a graduating high school senior, she entered the university with dreams of teaching music, but when a case of chronic laryngitis grew into vocal nodules, her career took an abrupt and unforeseen shift into the unknown. After exploring the many educational opportunities offered by the research university, Kayleigh graduated in May of 2013 with a bachelor of arts in psychology and minors in neuroscience and music. Kayleigh is pushing onward, reaching toward a career that will someday afford her the opportunity to enrich the experience of others, through either the field of psychology or education.

Ethan LaFrance is a student at the University of Pennsylvania, currently studying Middle Eastern studies and political science while growing a serious addiction to Philadelphia's many awesome food trucks. A lover of all things New Hampshire, Ethan has hiked the forty-eight four-thousand-footers in the White Mountains of his home state. When he's not rocking out to an eclectic mix of Bruce Springsteen, Zac Brown Band, and The Killers, Ethan can be found perusing the *Economist* or catching up on episodes of *Top Gear*. Ethan's academic passions range from health policy to national security issues, and he aspires to a life of serving the common good and seeking the joy of being alive.

Jennifer Lapp grew up on the Jersey Shore in Rumson, New Jersey. She pursued critical studies in film and television at the University of

Southern California's School of Cinematic Arts, with a minor in digital studies at the Institute for Multimedia Literacy, also in the cinema school. While at USC, Jennifer held internships at the Walt Disney Studios, Focus Features, and the *Hollywood Reporter*. She graduated in May 2014 and plans on pursuing a career in creative advertising or marketing in the film industry.

Tom Lehmann is a senior undergraduate student studying mathematics and biology at St. Lawrence University in upstate New York. He is from the small town of Sandwich, New Hampshire. He is active on campus, working as a mentor at the university's quantitative resource center, crew chief on the campus EMS squad, climbing instructor at the indoor climbing wall, and trip leader for the outing club. He is currently studying movement dynamics of Peruvian army ants as a senior thesis and is applying to graduate schools in the field of mathematical and computational biology. His hobbies include hiking, rock climbing, white-water paddling, and playing the saxophone.

Lindsey Luker is an American studies major at Hamilton College. Native to New Hampshire, she hopes to write for travel magazines and eventually make a home in New England. When she's not studying or working at the greenhouse, Lindsey can be found on the water with her two black Labs.

Gabriella Malek is a student at George Washington University, as well as an aspiring athlete and performer. In her youth, Gabriella was a Broadway and TV actress, featured in *Les Misérables*, *Chitty Chitty Bang Bang*, and the Nickelodeon TV show *The Backyardigans*. Her love of acting led to her involvement in the charity Broadway Kids Care, an organization comprising young actors dedicated to giving back to their community by means of volunteering and fund-raising. As a founding member, Gabriella has spoken at international events such as the Clinton Global Initiative, and for major organizations such as UNICEF.

In her free time, Gabriella volunteers as an EMT and sails as a Division I athlete. Following her continued commitment to helping others and inspired by her valuable experience as an EMT and singer, she has decided to pursue studies in premed and music.

Manda Marie is from a rural New Hampshire town. Her essay was written while she participated in the Advanced Study Program of the St. Paul's School, where she was inspired by her teachers and interns to challenge herself in her writing. The program helped her realize that she wants to pursue a career in the writing field. After college Manda intends to continue her writing career in the future with the hope that she can eventually write a novel.

C. H. Martin grew up in New Hampshire, and graduated from high school in 2009. He then attended Rensselaer Polytechnic Institute (RPI) in Troy, New York, to study physics. In the winter of 2012, he graduated with a bachelor's degree in physics and is now continuing his education at RPI in pursuit of his PhD in physics with a concentration in astronomy and astrophysics. In his spare time, he enjoys playing in the school pep band and operating the RPI observatory for public use every weekend.

Carolyn P. currently lives in Seattle, Washington, but lived in New Jersey through eighth grade. She now attends Emory University (class of 2018) on a merit scholarship.

Spencer Pallas is from Rochester, New Hampshire, and attended Northeastern University, majoring in mechanical engineering with a business minor. He works for a biomedical company in central Massachusetts and hopes to start his own company one day. When Spencer is not working, he loves to bike, play hockey, or go fishing with his dog Buckingham "Bucky" Pallas.

Claire Perry was raised on the New Jersey coast and recently moved to the Pacific Northwest. She graduated from Haverford College in 2014 with a major in economics and a minor in environmental science. She was a member of the Microfinance Consulting Club and helped map access to finance in Philadelphia and Ghana. Claire's studies focused on development economics and she spent two summers interning at Grameen Foundation. She likes hiking, traveling, and spending time with her extended family in Rockport, Massachusetts.

Sarah R. is from a tiny New Hampshire town with no traffic lights and one gas station. She attended Mount Holyoke College, a top-ranked liberal arts college in South Hadley, Massachusetts, and the oldest women's college in the country. Sarah double majored in English and philosophy and graduated *magna cum laude* with an honors thesis in May 2013. Her thesis was translations of the Old English epic poem *Judith* in both poetry and prose accompanied by a critical introduction and annotations. She is a member of Phi Beta Kappa and served as the copy chief for her college newspaper, the *Mount Holyoke News*. Sarah now works part time as the programming coordinator for her local library while running her own tutoring business. She is still actively applying for editorial positions in the Boston-area publishing industry. Ideally, she would like to be a full-time writer, focusing on young adult novels.

Adam Rice was born and raised in New Hampshire and went to a medium-sized high school. He graduated *cum laude* from Rensselaer Polytechnic Institute for computer science in 2013. He is currently living in Connecticut and works for Tata Consultancy Services as a software engineer. Since middle school, his main interest has been computers, but he was not able to write well. Adam wrote his essay while attending St. Paul's School's Advanced Studies Program (ASP) during the summer before eleventh grade. ASP had a class where he learned to write in the first-person narrative style. As a stereotypical "left-brained" person, he found that the writing class proved invaluable for his college applications. It also taught Adam that writing could can actually be fun.

Jac Stewart graduated in 2014 from Bates College, where he was a double major in philosophy and politics and president of the Brooks Quimby Debate Council and Philosophy Forum. He is also the cofounder of Money Out, an initiative bringing together young progressive activists working on issues adversely affected by the American campaign-finance system. Jac's interests include American pragmatist philosophy and progressive political activism, particularly regarding income inequality, government transparency, and campaign-finance reform. He also enjoys trail running, humor writing, and reading contemporary fiction. Jac has lived in New Hampshire, Maine, Manhattan, Brooklyn, and France.

Sean Thammakhoune grew up in Manchester, New Hampshire. He attends Rensselaer Polytechnic Institute (class of 2018) and plans to earn a PhD. In his free time, Sean enjoys looking for new ways to redesign ordinary items and playing golf, tennis, and hockey.

Robbie Trocchia was raised in Fair Haven, New Jersey, and graduated from Vassar College in Poughkeepsie, New York, with a degree in American studies.

Megan Walcek grew up in Dover, New Hampshire, where she attended Dover Senior High School. She is a member of the Harvard University class of 2015, concentrating in human evolutionary biology with a secondary field in global health and health policy. With an interest in nonprofits, she aspires to a career in public health or administrative health care. Megan enjoys watching sports and playing basketball, along with a creative interest in photography and event planning.

David F. White is from Hampton Falls, New Hampshire. He currently attends Colby College and will graduate in 2015. At Colby, he majors in economics and minors in East Asian studies and cinema studies. David is a member of the cross-country and track teams. David would like to extend thanks to Gregory Lawless for his encouragement and guidance as a friend and writing mentor.

Michaelle Yeo is from Moultonborough, New Hampshire, and is currently enrolled at Bowdoin College, class of 2016. She is working toward a bachelor's degree in government and history.

The author of "Good-Byes" was born and raised in New Hampshire. He attended Duke University and graduated in 2012 with BAs in history and Slavic and Eurasian studies. He currently attends Harvard Law School and anticipates graduating in 2016. He enjoys Italian cooking and playing guitar.

The author of "Off the Table" is a South Korean–born New Jerseyan, currently attending Princeton University (class of 2016). He intends to major in the Woodrow Wilson School of Public and International Affairs with certificates in Near Eastern studies and creative writing. His core academic interests include international conflict, Middle Eastern diplomacy, and American education policy. In his free time, he enjoys writing and performing spoken word poetry as part of Princeton's Ellipses Slam Poetry Group.

ACKNOWLEDGMENTS

Any compilation of writing requires the good will of many more people than does the average book, so there are many people to thank. My gratitude goes to the young writers whose generosity and openness made this project viable. Working with them on this book has been my distinct pleasure, and reading their stories gives me hope for the future.

Many people associated, past and present, with St. Paul's School Advanced Studies Program (ASP) in Concord, New Hampshire, have been extremely kind in facilitating contributions to this book: Michael S. Ricard; Joyce Ashcroft; Gregory and Jen Lawless; Marissa Schwalm; Kelly Hood; Sara Erdmann; and Jeff Baum, who is due recognition for the original idea of the narrative-lyric analogies chart.

ASP's need-blind work with New Hampshire's high school students merits praise, contribution, and emulation nationwide.

College Summit is a national nonprofit that does admirable college-preparedness outreach and is deserving of wide support as well.

I am also grateful to the community of Biotechnology High School (BTHS) in Freehold, New Jersey, especially to Dr. Linda Eno and Michelle Lampinen for letting me share with readers some of the wonderful materials that have served their students so well. My thanks also go to Dong and Mi Oh for their friendship and faith in this work, and to Heidi Griffith for her enthusiasm. My appreciation and respect to T. E. Lindner for steady guidance and insight over many years.

The people at Sourcebooks have been very kind and supportive throughout this first-publication experience. Thanks especially to Katherine Pidde for her calm and sure direction in editing and developing this book after acceptance, and to Michelle Lecuyer, who saw the work to completion. I'd like to thank others at Sourcebooks for their support of and involvement with this project: Dominique Raccah, Todd Stocke, Sean Murray, Chris Bauerle, Suzanna Bainbridge, Lindsay Newton, Rachel Kahn, and Melanie Jackson. Thank you to Sabrina Baskey-East for copyediting and to Barbara Hague for proofreading the book. To the other project contributors not named here, equally my appreciation.

Finally, I wish to thank my family and close friends of all varieties for their encouragement and support along the slow road through publishing, graduate studies, and life: my parents, Ann and Bob Wynne, Karen De Vries, Barbara Weitkamp, Marjee Ellis-Dean, Nick Ellis, Kristin Wynne, Dan Ramirez, Karin Wynne Cole, Michael Cole, and all in our extended East Coast clan. Finally, my love and deep gratitude to my wife Lauren Wynne and our sons Henry and William for keeping me honest and for making our life together so rich.

About the Author

A native of Southern California, Justin Nevin holds degrees from UC Santa Barbara and The University of Chicago. He has taught literature and writing at the high school and college levels for eight years and began advising college applicants in 2007. Interested in academic studies of literature, writing, and education, he is now working toward a doctorate at Binghamton University. He lives with his family in New York's Mohawk Valley.

NOTES

Notes

NOTES

NOTES

NOTES